WHAT READEI

"The better I know Michael Blue, the more I appreciate how much thought he's given to what it means to follow Jesus. Michael is insightful, honest, and sensitive to Christ and his kingdom priorities. In *Free to Follow*, he gives a Christ-centered wake-up call that can help you lose your life, and in the process, find it."

   – RANDY ALCORN, author of *Money, Possessions and Eternity, Managing God's Money and The Treasure Principle*

"I've written many endorsements in my professional career but this one is truly unique as I get to endorse a book written by my son. I'll say that I'm probably more qualified to write this endorsement than anyone else as I've watched him grow up for over forty years and have seen his maturing significantly in his faith over those forty years. When I read the book I was convicted. I had to ask myself the question, Am I truly surrendered? Michael challenges us with no wiggle room. You'll be blessed and changed as you read and apply this book. I can attest like no one else that he walks his talk and his mother and I are extremely proud to have watched him grow up to be the leader that he is. What a privilege to write this endorsement."

   – RON BLUE, author of *Master Your Money*, and founder of Ronald Blue Trust, Kingdom Advisors, and Ron Blue Institute

"An authentic, relatable journey into the depths of the gospel call to die to our ambitions and possessions. This biblically faithful work will draw you toward a richer, sweeter, and deeper walk in the way of Jesus."

   – JOHN CORTINES, author of *God and Money*, and Director of Generosity, Maclellan Foundation

"*Free to Follow* is an outstanding book! Michael Blue makes a compelling case for followers of Christ to surrender to him and wholeheartedly serve the Savior. It's extraordinarily well-written. This book will challenge you, convict you, and convince you that the path where you will discover ultimate joy and freedom is on the narrow road following Christ. I heartily recommend it!"

– HOWARD DAYTON, author of *Your Money Counts*,
and founder of Compass—finances God's Way

"The way of Jesus is hard to locate in modern times. It's even harder to navigate, so few attempt it. With remarkable clarity and biblical wisdom, Michael Blue points the way to life and unimaginable freedom and peace."

– GARY G. HOAG, author of *The Choice*,
President & CEO, Global Trust Partners

"This book serves as a great reminder, to all Christians, that God desires each of us to leverage our resources to meet urgent spiritual and physical needs around the world."

– CHRIS HUNSBERGER, CEO, Radical

"As I read this book I experienced a clear and challenging call to a life of surrender. Yet I didn't lose hope. Michael doesn't pull punches on how wealth, our materialistic culture, and even our churches can stand in the way of surrender. But he also shows through Scripture, stories, and practices of what a life of surrender to the ways of Jesus looks like, especially in our possessions and lifestyles. This book is full of grace and truth."

– PATRICK JOHNSON, founder of GenerousChurch

"In *Free to Follow*, Michael Blue deeply explores the implications of Jesus's call to find our highest and deepest satisfaction not in the gifts, but in the Giver—the need to die to self when it comes to money so that we might grasp hold of the greater gift of relationship with Jesus himself. Michael shares his own journey—warts and all—in growing in obedience that leads to radically countercultural joy. Readers will find themselves challenged and confronted, but will find in *Free to Follow* a compassionate companion for the difficult journey of disentangling our hearts from our wallets."

– **TIM MACREADY, Chief Investment Officer, Brightlight Group**

"Rooted firmly in biblical truth, this wisdom packed book has helped me see clearly how to approach finances so that they are not a stumbling block, or idol, but rather a tool for eternal riches. I know first-hand, that Michael Blue not only speaks, but demonstrates faith, generosity, and financial freedom with his life. Highly recommended for all of us in the West inundated by materialism, consumerism, and individualism."

– **DREW SHIH, Pastor, Living Stones Christian Church in Silicon Valley**

Discover the Riches
of a Surrendered Life

MICHAEL BLUE

THIRSTY LAND PRESS
thirstylandpress.com

Free to Follow
First Edition: 2020
ISBN: 978-0-9998673-3-4

Published by Thirsty Land Press
5524 Bee Cave Road, B-3
Austin, TX 78746 U.S.A.

Our books may be purchased in bulk for promotional,
educational, or ministry use. Please contact Thirsty Land Press
by email at info@thirstylandpress.com.

Editor: Ivan Mesa
Cover and interior design by TLC Book Design,
TLCBookDesign.com;
Cover: Tamara Dever; Interior: Monica Thomas

The Library of Congress Cataloging-in-Publication Data
is available upon request.

All author's royalties given to charity.

Printed in the United States of America
10   9   8   7   6   5   4   3   2   1

TABLE OF CONTENTS

ACKNOWLEDGMENTS

I'M INDEBTED TO many faithful believers and their writings in all of my thinking and writing, but am particularly indebted to Randy Alcorn, Craig Blomberg, St. John Chrysostom, Gary Hoag, and David Platt. Each is so influential in my understanding of the subject matter of this book, that it's impossible for me to have not unintentionally passed something off as my own thinking that I first read or heard from them. I take comfort in knowing that none of us stand alone and none of our thoughts are absolutely original, since they (hopefully) originated with Scripture itself. Regardless, I want to give credit where credit is due, and each of these men deserve a lot of credit for what you'll read in various parts of this book.

I'm grateful for the dear brothers who provided insightful, meaningful, and formative feedback on the development of this book: Phil Christensen, Phil Gelatt, Gary Hoag, Greg Hurley, Scott Rhodes, and Drew Shih.

Each of these men love Jesus passionately and have influenced my life more than words can express. All I can say is thank you!

I'm thankful for my parents and for the way they've been seeking God and growing toward him throughout their whole lives. Thank you for loving me, encouraging me, and, most importantly, modeling a life committed to following Jesus.

Finally, I can't adequately express my love for my family. My wife, Melissa, and our three boys, Nathan, Daniel, and Brooks. You'll see them throughout this book as a part of the story that I can't help but share as we journey together. I'm grateful that they've gone with me on this journey even when the path didn't seem certain and I didn't lead well. This is our story in the midst of God's greater story and will forever be written together. I can't think of four people I'd rather be journeying together with. I love you all with my whole heart!

INTRODUCTION

JESUS HATH NOW many lovers of his heavenly kingdom, but few bearers of his cross. He hath many desirous of comfort, but few of tribulation. He findeth many companions of his table, but few of his abstinence. All desire to rejoice with him, few are willing to endure anything for him, or with him. Many follow Jesus unto the breaking of bread; but few to the drinking of the cup of his passion. Many reverence his miracles, few follow the ignominy of his cross. Many love Jesus so long as adversities do not happen. Many praise and bless him, so long as they receive comforts from him.[1]

This was me. I was counted with the many. I'm ashamed to admit that a man living in the fifteenth century, Thomas à Kempis, put a pin so precisely on my life. The

---

1. Thomas à Kempis, *The Imitation of Christ* (c. 1418–1427; repr., Chicago: Moody, 2007), part 2, chap. 11, Kindle.

comforts of a Christian life were my lifelong companion, but I knew little of following in the way of Jesus.

My name is Michael Blue. You probably don't know me, but you may know my father—Ron Blue. My father is a well-known (at least to those who are older than fifty) Christian financial author, speaker, and entrepreneur. He literally wrote the book on managing personal finances from a biblical perspective.[2] As a child, my four siblings and I served as his test subjects. It was like living in a weird financial laboratory. We were weaned on the envelope system of managing money and each saved enough money by the age of sixteen to pay for half of our first car. Debt was a dangerous four-letter word and tithing was the unquestioned starting point for giving. Simply put, we knew how to be responsible with money. And we knew how to do it biblically.

Fast-forward to age thirty. I've been married eight years, have two children, and have been working as a big-firm attorney for four years. We live in a nice house 2.5 miles from downtown Austin, Texas. We belong to a church, attend regularly, tithe faithfully, save diligently, and, from all worldly external measures, are prospering. We were living the catalog version of the successful, sweet Christian life. But there was a problem. I was spiritually empty. Going through the motions. Questioning my faith. Frankly, I didn't need God in my life. He was nice for staying out of hell, but otherwise, he didn't serve much purpose. I had taken care of pretty much everything

---

2. Ron Blue, *Master Your Money: A Step-by-Step Plan for Experiencing Financial Contentment*, 5th ed. (Chicago: Moody, 2016).

else. Retirement, life insurance, disability insurance, college funding—it was all under control. The only thing I needed God for was a salve for my soul. And if that was all he was good for, was he even necessary?

So I began to search. Did I believe this stuff about God? With all that science had uncovered, could I believe in God? Was he necessary to understand the universe? What purpose did he serve in my life?

As I pondered these questions, I realized my view of God was flawed. My life with God was just like the "many" Thomas à Kempis described. He was someone I was associating with for my comfort and ease, but I had no understanding of what it meant to follow him. I didn't know God. I couldn't identify with the "few" Thomas à Kempis described. And I didn't want to. I came to the humbling conclusion that my life showed I didn't care about the things God cared about. I had satisfactorily checked the tithing box, but that was where it ended. I lived for entertainment, comfort, protection, and leisure. My life may have looked "Christian" from the outside, but in truth I looked nothing like Jesus. My heart was far from him.

This was the moment that brought me face-to-face with a devastating conclusion—I didn't believe the things about Jesus I claimed to believe. If I did, my life would ooze forth manifestations of that belief. Not just in a few external gestures, but in deep desperation of knowing him and making his name known. This realization forced me to make a choice. Either start living my life as if Jesus is who he said he is or quit playing religion and get on with my life. Being stuck in the middle was a reality I refused to wallow in any longer. As you might've guessed, I chose the former. I chose to take off my man-made yoke of religion and pick up Jesus's yoke. I decided it was time to quit playing at religion and start following Jesus.

And so my search became a journey, one that is still being written. A journey of learning to live a life testifying to the fact that God is a God who can still be trusted. And not just for eternity. This journey has forced me to radically rethink my life. It has taken me far outside my comfort zone and brought new life to my dying faith. For the first time, I understand what Jesus meant when he said to save my life I must lose it—what Thomas à Kempis meant when he described the "few" who take Jesus's invitation seriously. And this is now what I want. We've been learning surrender and trust as a family. It's been beautiful and messy and hard. But death is always hard. But with God, we're promised that death brings life. And that life is the only life worth pursuing. It's the life the "few" are privileged to live.

I want to invite you on a journey with the few. Where we explore what it means to lose our lives following Jesus. Where we learn why the way of the few is far better than the way of the many. Even in hardship. Especially in hardship.

The invitation to follow Jesus is a hard call, and few find it. But it's a good call. It's the only call that leads to life. I want us to dive deep into troubled waters and disrupt our preconceived notions of what it means to follow Jesus, particularly as it relates to our money.

Money is one of the key barriers preventing us from living a fully surrendered life. Much of this stems from how we view money and its purpose in our lives. We've been shaped by the culture around us and become convinced that money is a resource we're entitled to use for any purpose. This mentality has warped the way we relate to God and is keeping us from freely following Jesus. I want us to explore how to lay down this weight and burden in order to live the free life of a surrendered follower of Jesus.

We'll begin this journey by exploring Jesus's call to surrender and what that kind of life entails. We'll look specifically at what the Bible teaches about surrender in our finances. Then we'll turn to the great barrier to a surrendered life and explore the ways our churches have dressed this barrier up in Christian clothes leading us to believe it's right and good. Next, we'll look at what our response to the physical and spiritual urgencies in the world testifies to others about what we believe. Finally, we'll close with a call to live distinctly and pursue God with our lives.

These are questions which followers of Jesus have wrestled with since the beginning. I take solace in the consistent witness on this topic as I seek to exhort us to live fully surrendered lives. I want us to take seriously the call of Christ. I want us to think deeply about this call. Sadly, all too many of us live in the shallows of faith; I want us to live in the middle of the ocean. I want to call us out of the shallows and into the deep.

Are you ready to leave the safety of the shallows?

CHAPTER ONE

ASHAMED OF THE GOSPEL

"GOSPEL" MEANS GOOD NEWS.

That is why we call the story about Jesus Christ the "gospel."[1] It's good news. In fact, it's the best news in the world. As the apostle Paul described it, "I am not ashamed of the gospel, for it is the power of God for salvation to everyone who believes, to the Jew first and also to the Greek" (Rom. 1:16). The gospel is God's power to save *all* who believe. What better news could there ever be?

One thing has always struck me as odd in this verse: if this is such good news, why would Paul need to make it clear that he wasn't ashamed of it? Good news, by its nature, is welcome. Good things are worth sharing with others. So, why be ashamed of something good? Before

---

1. For more theological unpacking of the gospel, see Paul Washer, *The Gospel of Jesus Christ* (Grand Rapids, MI: Reformation Heritage, 2016).

answering that, let's look at another example of good news and how people responded to it.

On August 14, 1945, Japan unconditionally surrendered. World War II was over. As President Truman finished announcing this news to a throng of reporters squeezed into the Oval Office, the reporters rushed out of his office, grabbed the official announcement, and began broadcasting the good news. Within minutes, the world knew the good news. The war was over. The killing would stop.

Millions of people flooded the streets of major cities and celebrated for days. We can all envision the scenes as we think of soldiers kissing women, ticker tape falling, and Times Square overflowing. No doubt, in smaller towns, neighbors gathered to spread the news and celebrate the end of the bloodshed. Their boys were coming home. This news was the type of news that made strangers into friends and friends into family.

Good news like this is too good not to share. No one worries that they will offend someone by knocking on their door and telling them the war is over. Nobody would say, "I am not ashamed of the news that World War II is over." Simply put, there is nothing to be ashamed of in sharing good news like this. So why does Paul need to preface his statement about the gospel by saying he isn't ashamed of it?

If the gospel is indeed the salvation everyone needs to be made right with God and it is only through this salvation that we can be made right with God, then the gospel is good news we should unashamedly share. In fact, this good news is infinitely better than the news about the end of World War II. Why would anyone ever be ashamed of sharing it?

There is one glaring difference between the good news of World War II ending and the good news of the gospel. With the former, people were hoping for a solution to a major problem that affected every part of their lives, and with the latter, people don't think there is a problem needing a solution. Many people reject the gospel as good news because they don't think there is anything they need to be saved from. As a matter of fact, the idea that they need saving is offensive to them. Knowing that people aren't looking for the good news of the gospel and may even be offended by the suggestion that they need to be saved from something, can create a sense of fear, or shame, for us when we want to share the gospel. This is why we might behave as if we're ashamed of the gospel.

I've spent much of my life wrestling with this sense of fear and shame. I know I should share the gospel with people, but I'm fearful of the possibility of experiencing social awkwardness or rejection. I get too concerned with the fear that if a person rejects my presentation of the gospel, they're also rejecting me and we'll never have a normal interaction again. As a result, I have far too often failed to share the gospel. I have lived as one who is ashamed of the gospel.

I don't think I'm alone in this.

I believe most of us have experienced this shame and felt guilty over our failed attempts to overcome it. I'm convinced the only way we will ever overcome this fear is by rightly understanding the magnitude of the good news of the gospel. News that is so good it makes the good news of the end of World War II look like news that there is a $0.01 discount on a cup of coffee at the gas station. Putting the gospel's saving power into proper perspective allows us to overwhelm our feelings of shame and fear with the magnificence of its power. It is incumbent on each of us to bask in the unspeakable magnificence of the good news of the gospel and then share it with others regardless of how they may respond.

I believe these feelings of fear and shame are a major part of what Paul meant when he said he wasn't ashamed of the gospel. He wasn't going to fear telling anyone about it just because they didn't believe it or think they needed it. And the reason he could do this was that he deeply understood the saving power of the gospel.

DIFFERENT SHAME

While this type of shame is certainly a part of what Paul addresses, I believe there is another type of shame—a more insidious type—with which Paul is also concerned. A shame that poisons Christianity in the West, a shame that has become so complete that we now glorify its opposite. What is it?

It's being ashamed of the call of Christ.

The call to lose our lives, take up our crosses, and follow Jesus. And Paul says that in addition to not being ashamed to share the gospel, we shouldn't be ashamed of the gospel's call, which is the call of Christ. Unfortunately, instead of embracing this call, we seem to insist that a life following Jesus requires nothing from us. As long as we said a little prayer, raised a hand, or walked an aisle, we're good. We now can get all this life has to offer—*and* eternity thrown in. Best of all, we don't have to deny ourselves anything. We have become so ashamed of Christ's call, that we live as if there is no call.

But Jesus disagrees:

> *If anyone would come after me, let him deny himself and take up his cross daily and follow me. For whoever would save his life will lose it, but whoever loses his life for my sake will save it. For what does it profit a man if he gains the whole world and loses or forfeits himself? For whoever is ashamed of me and of my words, of him will the Son of Man be ashamed when he comes in his glory and the glory of the Father and of the holy angels. (Luke 9:23b–26)*

Do you see it? Jesus tells us not to be ashamed of him or his words.

Which words? That following Jesus requires us to deny ourselves, take up our crosses, go wherever he leads, quit trying to gain the world, and lose our lives. This is the call of Christ. And he tells us not to be ashamed of it. Paul paints the same picture in his second letter to Timothy:

> *Therefore do not be ashamed of the testimony about our Lord, nor of me his prisoner, but share in suffering for the gospel by the power of God, who*

saved us and called us to a holy calling, not because of our works but because of his own purpose and grace, which he gave us in Christ Jesus before the ages began, ... for which I was appointed a preacher and apostle and teacher, which is why I suffer as I do. But I am not ashamed, for I know whom I have believed, and I am convinced that he is able to guard until that day what has been entrusted to me. (2 Tim. 1:8–12)

Christ's call took Paul through prison and suffering. Paul viewed his suffering as a part of his call. A part that validated his faith and ministry. From this perspective, Paul tells us not to be ashamed of Jesus's call and what it will almost certainly lead to. This is the "shame" of the gospel. The reality we try to sweep under the rug and ignore. The counter-cultural call to deny ourselves, take up our crosses, and follow Jesus. It isn't just that we've failed to teach this truth, it's that we have taught the exact opposite. We have taught that the gospel requires nothing from us. That it is a gateway to comfort. A gateway to happiness. A gateway to health, wealth, and prosperity.

Now don't let yourself off the hook too quickly when you see the words "health, wealth, and prosperity." Don't think that just because you say you abhor the prosperity gospel that it isn't codified in your heart. If the call to follow Jesus entails losing your life, what part of your life have you lost for him? What part of your life is your church calling you to lose in pursuit of Jesus? It isn't just your old sinful ways. It's all of you.

As C. S. Lewis explains, Jesus says, "Give me all. I don't want so much of your time and so much of your money and so much of your work: I want You. I have not come to torment your natural self, but to kill it."[2]

This is a hard calling and the stakes are high. We can't afford to get this wrong. Look again at what Jesus says after he calls us to follow, "For whoever is ashamed of me and of my words, of him will the Son of Man be ashamed when he comes in his glory" (Luke 9:26a). If we're ashamed of the call of Jesus—of the call to lose our lives—then Jesus tells us that he too will be ashamed of us when he comes again to judge the world. This isn't a little thing. This is, in fact, everything. We can't get this wrong. Jesus tells us there is a high cost in being ashamed of the call to follow Jesus—the call to lose our lives.

Are you ashamed of this call? Do you believe a life following Jesus is worth losing everything you hold dear in your life?

TWO RESPONSES TO THE CALL OF CHRIST

Two stories from the Bible will help us more honestly evaluate our answers to these questions. As we read these stories, let's ask ourselves which person we'd rather be?

The first story comes from Mark 10. In this story, a rich young man runs up to Jesus, kneels before him,

---

2. C. S. Lewis, *Mere Christianity*, rev. ed. (New York: Macmillan, 1960), 153.

and asks him what he needs to do to inherit eternal life. Jesus begins by telling him to obey the commandments. This man boldly declares that he has kept all of the commandments since he was young—which Jesus sidesteps. And then we read,

> *And Jesus, looking at him, loved him, and said to him, "You lack one thing: go, sell all that you have and give to the poor, and you will have treasure in heaven; and come, follow me." Disheartened by the saying, he went away sorrowful, for he had great possessions.* (Mark 10:21–22)

Here you have a man concerned with his eternal soul who had lived a righteous life. And, Jesus, instead of commending him for his righteous living, tells him that he lacks something. Whatever this lack was, the way for him to overcome it was to sell everything he owned and give it to the poor. If he obeyed, Jesus would welcome him as one of his followers.

The second story comes from Matthew 13:44. In this story, there's a man taking a walk. As he stops to rest in a field, he uncovers a hidden treasure worth more than anything he has ever seen. Quickly looking around to make sure nobody is watching, he reburies the treasure and hurries to find the owner of the field. Upon finding the field's owner, he inquires about the price of the field and immediately realizes that if he sells everything he owns, he'll have just enough to buy the field. And he does.

The Bible tells the story this way: "The kingdom of heaven is like treasure hidden in a field, which a man found and covered up. Then in his joy he goes and sells all that he has and buys that field" (Matt. 13:44).

Who would you rather be? The man in the first or the second story? Even the mood of the stories points us to the man in the second story. The second story says the man sold everything he had to buy the field "in his joy." Whereas, it says the man in the first story "went away sorrowful, for he had great possessions." The man in the second story ends up with a massive treasure, while the man in the first story is asked to dispose of his.

This is where we get a chance to see whether our hearts really think that following Jesus and eternity are worth losing our lives. As you consider which man you'd rather be, I'd like to ask a question: what's different about these stories?

In each story, the men are seeking eternity.

In each story, the cost of eternity is everything they owned.

I believe these stories are fundamentally the same story. They're practically identical. Yet, for some reason, we look at the story of the first man and feel sorry for him. Why? It even says in the story that Jesus looked at him and *loved* him. That means Jesus considered what was best for this guy—as we all would do for someone whom we loved. So, why do I feel sorry for him and why did he walk away sad? On the flip side, why do I not feel sorry for the second guy when he had to sell all his stuff and why was he able to do it with such joy?

It comes down to how we view eternity. Do we see eternity as immeasurably valuable such that there is no cost we would be unwilling to pay for it? Or, do we see eternity as a hoped-for reality, but not one we're willing to sacrifice much for?

I believe the reason we feel sorry for the first man is we're ashamed of the call of the gospel. We want the promise (eternity) without the call (now). We're not even convinced that the promise is worth the call. We certainly don't live like we believe eternity is worth losing our lives over. Bluntly put, we have a low view of God and eternity. We don't believe that getting to be with God for eternity is vastly superior to all the world offers. We don't even believe it's a little bit superior. When Jesus tells us to lose our lives to follow him, our first thought is—the cost is too high. We'd rather keep this world than gain the next.

To make this even harder, we live in a world intent on making us love it and disregard everything else. And to a large extent, the world has been far more effective at making disciples than we have. With the constant deluge of advertising, branding, self-exaltation, and a general promise of finding a soul-satisfying life in this world, we're being discipled with the message that this world is the best we could ever want or need. This message has been intentional and methodical. So, like a frog being boiled in a slowly heated pot of water, we're being subtly discipled into a love for this world. As Screwtape wrote to Wormwood, "Indeed the safest road to Hell is the gradual one—the gentle slope, soft underfoot, without sudden turnings, without milestones, without signposts."[3] And as a result, without noticing what's happening we've come to believe this world is our home—that this world will satisfy our souls and any call to lose any part of it is too costly.

THE CALL IS COSTLY

The thing about belief is that it is costly—at least from the perspective of this world. It's a call to come and die to ourselves. It'll make us uncomfortable since it'll root out anything we treasure over Christ. We must die to these idols. And when we die to anything, it hurts. But one thing I know about the gospel is that following every death there is resurrection. Our death to these idols leads us to life.

In many churches today you can attend every Sunday and never hear the call of Christ. The call to lose your life. The call to die to the idols of the culture and to die to yourself. Many pastors are silent about the multitude of warnings relating to wealth and greed, even though Jesus warns about greed ten to twenty times more than any other sin.[4] Instead, you're more likely to see the idols of the culture celebrated and lauded as rewards for godly living. You'll be told that God must really be

3. C. S. Lewis, *The Screwtape Letters* (1942; repr., San Francisco: HarperOne, 2015), 60.

4. Timothy Keller, "The Gospel, Grace, and Giving," November 19, 2015, Vimeo, 16:00, https://vimeo.com/146255187.

pleased with you because he has given you so much of the world's treasure to enjoy. Further, you'll be told that if you raised your hand, prayed a prayer, or walked an aisle, then you're saved. But if you look at people's lives after such events you often see no change, no evidence of belief, no fruit. Instead, you see a deep and unyielding love of self and the world.

When you ask most people in a church what Christianity is all about, you'll likely hear answers such as, "Jesus saves me," "Jesus forgives me," and "Jesus loves me." Of course, none of these answers is entirely wrong, but there is a subtle problem with each of them. Who is the object of these sentences? I am. But you and I aren't the focal point of the Christian faith. Christ is. When we treat Christianity like this it turns Christ into our ticket out of hell instead of our treasure for eternity. Jesus saves me, forgives me, and loves me *so that* his name would be known on the earth (Ps. 67). It isn't for me, it's for him. That's the point of Christianity.

Merely to believe that Jesus is God will do us no good in eternity. The book of James tells us that even the demons believe Jesus is God and shudder (James 2:19). I fear demons have more belief in God than many who fill up a church on Sunday. They not only believe Jesus is God, they shudder at his power. They know that if a person comes face to face with God in his full divinity and power they will be changed. Because when we come face to face with the God who created the universe it changes us.

Please don't misunderstand me. I'm not saying salvation can be earned. Salvation is by grace alone through faith alone in Christ alone. This isn't us doing enough to prove our belief; it's us coming face to face with God and believing he is who he says he is—believing he is trustworthy and worth our lives. That Jesus's work on the cross alone saves us. An understanding of this grace and the work of Christ transforms the way we respond to the call of Jesus. The only proper response to salvation is the response of the second man—joyfully losing our lives for the gospel. We'll certainly not do this perfectly, but this type of belief will always cause our heart to move toward this end.

The call of the gospel isn't easy. The way is narrow. I fear that until we can say with Paul, "I count everything as loss because of the surpassing worth of knowing Christ Jesus my Lord. For his sake I have suffered the loss of all things and count them as rubbish, in order that I may gain Christ" (Phil. 3:8), that we're merely playing games with Christianity. We may want to use Christ to gain eternal life, but we don't want Christ for Christ's sake. Paul valued Christ and wanted nothing more than to be in his presence. He was willing to pay any price, including his life, for this one simple thing.

Let me ask you again. Are you ashamed of Christ's call? Are you embarrassed by Paul's dedication? Are you willing to lose your life for Jesus? Are you willing to lose it all just to know God more?

RICH MAN'S RESPONSE

Let's return to the story of the rich young man. In this story, after Jesus asks him to sell everything, he invites the man to follow him. Think about this invitation. It's an invitation to walk with Jesus, listen to him teach, eat with him, and rest with him. To simply be with Jesus while he walked the dusty roads of Galilee. This man is being offered the chance to walk with God's Son as his prelude to eternity—and his response is sorrow. Why? Because he had great possessions. Because what Jesus asked him to do was excruciatingly hard. And he wasn't convinced it was worth it.

So what did he do? "He went away sorrowful" (Mark 10:22b).

I've always assumed that his leaving in sorrow was tantamount to his rejection of Jesus. His final decision to keep his stuff and not follow Jesus. That in the end he missed the kingdom. The problem with this common assumption is nothing in the text tells us this is what actually happened. All it says is "he went away sorrowful." It's entirely possible this man went away sorrowful and then obeyed.[5] It's possible that his act of going away was his first act of obedience to Jesus's command for him to *go* and sell. We simply don't know.

As I've considered the possibility that the rich young man didn't ultimately reject Jesus, but was instead sorrowful because of the weight of Jesus's call,

---

5. Gary G. Hoag, *Wealth in Ancient Ephesus and the First Letter to Timothy: Fresh insights from Ephesiaca by Xenophon of Ephesus* (University Park, PA: Eisenbrauns, 2015), 218–20.

I've come to realize that I can relate to the rich young man much more than the joyful man. For much of my life I've seen the offer of eternity and a life of following Jesus as a difficult invitation to carefully consider. I've rarely responded like the second man with joyful abandonment rushing to sell everything to gain eternity. Instead, like the rich young man, I drop my shoulders and despair over the difficulty of the call, asking why it has to be so hard.

But I don't just relate to the rich young man, I am the rich young man. While I long to be the joyful man, for most of my life I've heard Christ's call and responded with sorrow. It has only been through slow, painstaking, begrudging obedience that I've grown to see the call to lose my life as a call to joy. A call to life. Perhaps this is the story of the rich young man as well. Perhaps, in the end, he sold it all and followed Jesus.

I don't think I'm alone in my response. I think many people read Jesus's call to the rich young man and think Jesus is asking too much. The cost is too high. But the good news is that Jesus knows his call is hard. He knows we'll see the cost as impossibly high. Look what Jesus says as the rich young man walks away: "How difficult it will be for those who have wealth to enter the kingdom of God" (Mark 10:23b). This isn't condemnation, it's compassion. Jesus loves this man and feels compassion as he walks away. And in this infinite compassion, Jesus acknowledges that his call is difficult. Even still, he doesn't diminish the call. He doesn't lower the bar. Instead, he promises that if we rely on him, he'll provide the way. He says, "With man it is impossible, but not with God. For all things are possible with God" (Mark 10:27b).

Then, Jesus shows us the joy awaiting us when we, through his power, respond to his call with obedience. He says when we obey his call we will "receive a hundredfold now in this time, houses and brothers and sisters and mothers and children and lands, with persecutions, and in the age to come eternal life" (Mark 10:30b). What a promise! What Jesus describes is God's kingdom and the community of all believers who walk the path of surrender. He doesn't say it'll become easy. He actually promises the opposite when he says "with persecutions"—but, he says it'll be worth it. One hundred times so. He says that when we align under our heavenly Father in abandoned obedience, we'll receive immeasurably more than what we gave up. In this age, we will be grafted into a community of Christ followers who have lost their lives for the sake of Christ; who have said everything I have has been given to me by God and is available to be used by God. This is the promise now. This is the community that fulfills his hundredfold promise. Not only that, he promises eternal life in the age to come—in the presence of God and his glory. Each of these promises draws us intimately into a deeper knowledge of God and his glory, both now and in eternity.

Understanding these truths allows us to move from the response of the rich man to the response of the joyful man. Understanding these truths and responding in obedience—even amid sorrowful obedience—is the only way we'll ever become free to follow in the way of Jesus.

CALL BEFORE US

This is the call before us. Will we deny ourselves, take up our crosses, and follow Jesus? Even if it means losing our lives? Will we obey even when it's hard to trust that the promise is better than what we already have? Are we willing to trust that when Jesus calls us to follow, he is calling us to real life? Are we willing to trust God that eternity, his kingdom, and the community of followers are infinitely better than any of our stuff? Are we willing to follow Jesus even if it appears impossibly hard?

When we understand who Jesus is, what he has done, and the promise of eternity, there is no idol, there is no thing in our lives, there is no price we must pay that seems costly.

Simply stated, if Jesus is worth anything, he's worth everything.

This is what this book is about. It's an invitation to take seriously the call to lose our lives. It's an invitation to things that seem hard but results in life that is indescribably sweet and nearer to God's presence. We'll look at the reality of our world and the importance of the church waking up and living unashamed of Christ's call. We'll delve into the question of what it means to lose our lives with regard to money and possessions. Living in one of the wealthiest nations in the history of the world, the pursuit and worship of wealth have been canonized in our culture and even in the church.

Do we truly believe that following God is worth our lives and our stuff? Are we willing to purge ourselves of the culture's idols to make God's name known in the world?

THE TRIP THAT TRANSFORMED OUR HEARTS

The rivalry raging in my heart between this world and the Lord came to a head a few years ago on a trip to East Africa with a relief organization called Crisis Aid. During this trip, my wife and I were privileged to see all the work being done to combat physical, emotional, and spiritual suffering. We saw feeding programs, hospitals in action, red light rescue operations, orphan care, well digging, and more.

We looked into the eyes of a mother who had walked twelve hours to get food for her child who was days away from starving to death. We cared for a widow who was on the brink of death and attempting to care for her two kids alone. As we walked into her home made up of a few sticks and a tarp, we surveyed all of her earthly belongings and all the food she had left, a half-eaten ear of burnt corn. We sat down with a woman confined to a room no larger than a closet, condemned to a life of prostitution, as she showed us pictures of her children, each of whom she had given up for adoption. We saw people sick and dying from simple, preventable diseases. We saw poverty on an extreme scale. It was shattering.

As we went from place to place and saw need after need, we couldn't shake the sense that God was asking us what we were going to do. He kept pointing us to the stockpile we were building in our savings and retirement accounts and asking us why we would hold on to that money for a day that may never come (retirement, an emergency, etc.) when the need before us is so present and urgent. It was as if the Lord was saying, "Why are you holding onto something for a future that is uncertain when the need before you is so certain?"

What would we do if any of these things were happening to one of our friends or family members? Why would we only consider these needs urgent if they were happening to people close to us? Wouldn't our love for God and our neighbor necessitate that we treat their urgent physical and spiritual needs as we would our own?[6]

These are the questions that have convicted and challenged me the last few years. I'd like to invite you into my journey as we wrestle with the question, "Are we willing to lose our lives for the sake of Jesus, and if we are, what does that mean?" I ask you to read with an open heart and mind as we explore the call of the gospel. There is joy and there is hope, but to get there we need to take a hard, difficult look at where we are.

---

6. You may protest that in a world of brokenness we can't possibly address everything gone wrong. While this is certainly true, I fear we all too often use that as an excuse to address very little. We'll explore this line of thinking in this book and examine whether we're using that as an excuse to do nothing or living in submission to God and his call in determining how, where, and when to help. We may not be able to respond to everything, but we can almost certainly respond more faithfully.

CHAPTER TWO

CALL TO SURRENDER

"**FOLLOW ME.**" These two words, at once, offer the most wonderful invitation and most terrifying call imaginable.

Jesus's call to follow him wasn't for the faint of heart.

Consider Peter. He received two calls, one at the beginning of Jesus's ministry and one at the end.

The first call comes following a bad night of fishing. Peter and his companions had fished all night and caught nothing. While they were dejectedly putting their fishing nets away, Jesus comes along, jumps in Peter's boat, and begins teaching people on the shore. After a bit, Jesus turns to Peter and offers him some fishing advice. He tells him to try again. To throw his nets out one more time. Peter must have been thinking, "Seriously? A carpenter giving me fishing advice? This isn't going to turn out well." After protesting, Peter relents, tosses his nets over the side of the boat, and pulls in a haul of fish more massive than anything he has ever seen. The catch of fish so astonishes Peter that he falls to his knees before Jesus. Jesus then looks at Peter (and his brother Andrew) and says, "Follow me, and I will make you fishers of men" (Matt. 4:19).[1]

At seeing their catch and hearing the call of Jesus, Peter and his brother don't hesitate. They leave everything and follow Jesus. All because an upstart rabbi invited them to follow.

Peter and Andrew very likely knew who Jesus was before this encounter. At a minimum, they would've heard rumors of his miracles, reports of his teaching, and speculation about who he might be. They almost certainly knew Jesus was an itinerant preacher, which meant he had no one place he called home. So, in following Jesus, they had to accept this itinerant lifestyle. They knew that Jesus's call to follow him meant leaving their jobs, sources of income, homes, and families as they traveled from place to place with Jesus. They knew following Jesus required them to live like he did and adopt his lifestyle.

Their response: "Immediately they left their nets and followed him" (Matt. 4:20). No hesitation. No looking back. At Jesus's call, they follow.

---

1. There are two recorded descriptions of this first call. One in Luke 5 and one in Matt. 4. It seems that these two stories most likely describe the same call and so I have assumed that they do. There are some scholars who think that there were two calls of Peter and Andrew. I don't believe that it makes much difference in how I am treating this passage one way or another. Particularly, since Jesus makes a similar invitation for Peter to follow him in Luke 5 as well.

That was Peter's first call. And while we should certainly commend Peter for his quick response, it doesn't appear that he fully understood Jesus's call. He no doubt knew that the call required him to give up his current life and live as Jesus lived. But, he also believed he'd gain personally and politically by following Jesus. So, while he abandoned much to follow Jesus, he didn't fully comprehend the cost Jesus was asking him to pay. This becomes clear as we fast forward to the events immediately preceding Peter's second call.

Peter's second call comes after Jesus's death and resurrection. It comes at a low point in Peter's life. Before Jesus is arrested, Peter boldly claims that he would follow Jesus all the way to death, exhibiting his continued belief that this whole thing was primarily about gaining political revolution. However, at the first sign of danger, Peter denies knowing Jesus—on three separate occasions. After Peter's denials, Jesus is tried, condemned, beaten, and crucified. Peter is nowhere to be found. When his life is on the line and the possibility of personal gain and political power vanishes, Peter runs away. Jesus had given Peter the opportunity to lose his life in following him and instead he disappears, demonstrating his total lack of understanding of Jesus's call.

As Peter is dealing with his crushing failure, Jesus rises from the grave and begins visiting his disciples, including Peter. I believe that at seeing Jesus, Peter is at once overjoyed and humiliated. He knows of his boast, his pride, and his failure. But he doesn't know what to do. So, he does what comes naturally—he goes fishing.

To add insult to uncertainty and humiliation, during the night of fishing, Peter and his companions catch nothing. They work all night and don't have a single fish to show for it. But then, Peter hears a familiar voice from the shore offering unsolicited fishing advice, telling him to try one more cast. Could it be? This scene is eerily reminiscent of Peter's first call. Could Jesus be calling him again? Peter obeys and throws the net in one more time. What happens? A haul of fish like nothing he had seen before. (Well, almost never—there was that one other time Jesus showed up with unsolicited fishing advice.) Peter is astonished yet again. Instead of hauling in the fish, he dives into the water and swims to Jesus.

Now, here is where this story gets intriguing. As Peter climbs out of the water, Jesus meets him and offers restoration and provides clarity to his call. He asks Peter three times if he loves him—the same number of times as Peter's denials. After Peter insists that he does, Jesus tells him to feed and shepherd his sheep. Shepherding wasn't a dream job for anyone. And Peter is told that following Jesus required him to be a shepherd of Jesus's sheep. No more just catching new sheep, he now must do the dirty work of caring for and training them. If this new job wasn't hard enough, Jesus makes it clear what the call to follow him actually means. If Peter chooses to follow Jesus, this time it *will* cost him his life. No aspirations of personal gain or political power can remain. No misconceptions are permitted in this call. If Peter follows, he will become a prisoner and ultimately die.

After everything has been made clear, Jesus extends a second call to Peter, "Follow me" (John 21:19).

UNDERSTANDING THE CALL

How does that invitation sound to you? "I am going to give you a nearly impossible job, you will be hated, you will be imprisoned, and you will die because of me." Not exactly the invitation you hear at many churches on Sunday mornings. Imagine your pastor standing up and saying, "God loves you and wants you to follow him today. He has an impossible task for you to do. He is promising that your way will be filled with suffering and persecution, and likely an early death. He's inviting you to lose your life today. Now come, accept this invitation, and follow Jesus."

This was the invitation Peter got both times. He didn't understand the cost fully the first time, but Jesus left no doubt the second time. The cost to follow was his life. The promised gain was becoming more like Jesus. This is the same invitation we're given to follow Jesus.

The primary word used by the Gospel writers which we translate as "follow" has the connotation of following a leader, coming behind, and becoming an apprentice. This means that when we follow someone, we'll walk as they walked and become more like them. So, when Jesus calls us to follow him, he's inviting us to walk in the way he walked; to imitate him and his lifestyle; and, ultimately, to become like him. After all, Jesus's followers should look like him.

When we understand that the call to *follow* entails the call to *become*, we can see why this call to follow Jesus requires us to give up pursuing our pleasures and personal gain. This call is costly. Jesus's call to follow isn't easy. It's a call to come and die to ourselves. Whether we understand this to be the case or not, implicit in every call of Jesus is the call to surrender. This is what Jesus helped Peter understand in his second call, and this is what we have the advantage of understanding as we look at Jesus's calls to follow him:

> *"Whoever loves father or mother more than me is not worthy of me, and whoever loves son or daughter more than me is not worthy of me. And whoever does not take his cross and follow me is not worthy of me." (Matt. 10:37–38)*

> *"If anyone comes to me and does not hate his own father and mother and wife and children and brothers and sisters, yes, and even his own life, he cannot be my disciple. Whoever does not bear his own cross and come after me cannot be my disciple. . . . So therefore, any one of you who does not renounce all that he has cannot be my disciple." (Luke 14:26–27, 33)*

> *Then Jesus told his disciples, "If anyone would come after me, let him deny himself and take up his cross and follow me. For whoever would save his life will lose it, but whoever loses his life for my sake will find it." (Matt. 16:24–25)*

> *As they were going along the road, someone said to him, "I will follow you wherever you go." And Jesus said to him, "Foxes have holes, and birds of the air have nests, but the Son of Man has nowhere to lay his head." To another he said, "Follow me." But he*

said, "Lord, let me first go and bury my father." And Jesus said to him, "Leave the dead to bury their own dead. But as for you, go and proclaim the kingdom of God." Yet another said, "I will follow you, Lord, but let me first say farewell to those at my home." Jesus said to him, "No one who puts his hand to the plow and looks back is fit for the kingdom of God."
(Luke 9:57–62)

When Jesus heard this, he said to him, "One thing you still lack. Sell all that you have and distribute to the poor, and you will have treasure in heaven; and come, follow me."
(Luke 18:22)

The calls to follow Jesus require extreme sacrifice. They require us to forsake everything. Even good things. Over and over in the Gospels, we see Jesus's followers leaving good things to follow him: businesses, family, homes, friends, community, influence, power, and more. Regardless of what they thought they were getting, Jesus's call was a call to forsake everything, start walking after him, and become like him. This cost of following Christ is so explicit throughout the New Testament that Paul could tell the Galatians that he had "been crucified with Christ" (Gal. 2:20). The call to follow Jesus isn't merely a call to kind of believe, it's a call to come and die.

A moderated religion is no religion at all. It seems there are few who take Jesus's call seriously. Too many of us are looking around at everyone else in our churches assuming that if we look like them we must be on the right path. There is a very real danger in judging our spiritual conditions by examining the lives of those around us who are just like us. Instead, we must ask ourselves if we're ready to follow Jesus, to give him our whole lives—to become like him—no matter the cost.

BEAUTY OF THE CALL

Does this call feel harsh? Does it feel unnecessarily hard? Let's remember what Jesus told us in Luke 9:24: "whoever loses his life for my sake will save it." We find our lives by losing them. What if this call was the one thing that could bring us everlasting joy? What if the reason it feels hard is that we have idols we cherish way too much, that we aren't ready to part with? Idols that are keeping us from knowing God fully and experiencing his presence completely. What if the reason it feels hard is that our hearts don't treasure knowing Jesus or experiencing his presence? We'd rather hold on to our idols than take hold of that which is truly life.

There is such beautiful promise in heeding this call and dying to our idols. When we do this, we experience a radical change in the things we love and treasure most. Paul said it this way: "Therefore, if anyone is in Christ, he is a new creation. The old has passed away; behold, the new has come" (2 Cor. 5:17).

When we follow Jesus, we become entirely new creations. Our loves change, our perspectives change, our desires change—everything changes. This is what Jesus invites us to. He invites us to become something new—to be like him, to love what he loves, to live as he lived, to walk in the way he walked. A life following in the way of Jesus brings about new life as our old lives die.

Paul understood more than most what it meant to become something new. Paul went from a self-righteous accomplice to murder and persecutor of Jesus's followers to an appointed apostle. When Paul says he was the chief of sinners (1 Tim. 1:15), he wasn't being falsely humble; he meant it. The things he did to the church were horrible. Paul knew God had every right to wipe him out, but instead he gave Paul new life as a new creation. In understanding this grace, Paul was willing to go wherever God sent him and suffer whatever he must suffer. Paul had seen clearly where he had come from and what he had been called to. He weighed the difference and the choice to lose his life for Jesus became the most logical choice imaginable. This new life is what Jesus offered to the rich young man and what he showed his disciples. It is worth more than we can fathom, but to find it we must follow. We must answer the call of Jesus. In his strength, we must take the first hard steps of following, trusting that the end is joy. We must see our sin in all its horror and trust the call of the one who delivered us.

PARTIAL CALL?

Is this the call to follow you're answering? Or are you pursuing God for your personal gain, like Peter first did? Do you say that you're following Jesus, but your loves remain unchanged? If so, there's a problem.

Think about it like this: imagine you're one of those people who always has a girlfriend. You don't just date either. You date in that over the top, romantic, mushy, touchy-feely way. You post about your current love all the time on social media, introduce them to everyone, and always seem head over heels in love with whoever you're dating. Then one day you meet the person you actually want to marry. You date for a while, get engaged, have a beautiful wedding, and go on a romantic fourteen-day honeymoon to an island paradise. After the honeymoon, you get home and over time start hanging out with some of your old girlfriends. You start posting about them on social media. You call and text them regularly. You even go out with some of them on the weekends. How would your wife react?

I'm guessing she'd be less than pleased. She'd probably throw you out. What if you protested and insisted that you loved her, you just weren't ready to let go of your other lovers? Then, you showed her your wedding ring and told her how you never took it off. You reminded her that you still lived with her and came home almost every night. Not just that, but you even begin to brag how you tell most people you meet that you're married ... to her. Finally, you remind her how you buy her things on her birthday, Valentine's Day, your anniversary, and Christmas. You never miss being with her on those special days.

You may appear married from the outside, but if you've never severed ties with your old loves, then you haven't committed to your marriage. This isn't the picture of marriage that anyone would recommend. This isn't a marriage that will last. When you become one with your wife, your old loves better become dead to you. If they don't, your marriage is the thing that will die.

Now imagine this on an infinite scale. The Creator of the universe, in his invitation to follow him, requires you to die to self by dying to all other loves. This isn't an unreasonable request, just like it isn't unreasonable for your wife to expect you to reject all your old girlfriends. It's the only way to live logically and consistently with your newly declared love. If you're pursuing the way of Jesus and have become a new creation, how could anything else steal your gaze? If you've understood God's grace and what you've been saved from and to, how could you live with anything but abandoned gratitude? How could you even want to let your old loves linger? They won't satisfy. They can't satisfy. As a matter of fact, the only thing they can do is destroy your relationship with God. If the only thing that an old love can do is destroy your relationship, you'd be a fool to let it linger.

Cut it off. Renounce it. Die to it.

CALL TO SURRENDER

Are you ready to abandon your old loves? Are you ready to follow Jesus? To do so, you must surrender everything you love, everything you have, and everything you are to him. This is the call. This is the new life you're invited into. This is what the Bible calls surrender. This is what

Jesus modeled when he walked on earth. This is the way of Jesus.

If you want to follow Jesus and walk in his way, you must live as he lived. And he lived a life of surrender and submission. Philippians 2:6–8 tells us that Jesus, "though he was in the form of God, did not count equality with God a thing to be grasped, but emptied himself, by taking the form of a servant, being born in the likeness of men. And being found in human form, he humbled himself by becoming obedient to the point of death, even death on a cross."

If Jesus walked the road of surrender and submission, then this should be the same road that we walk. This isn't a call to doom and gloom—but to joy and peace. This is the only place where we can find our lives. We'll talk plenty about the joy of following Jesus in this book, but for now, I want to awaken us to the truth that we've been ashamed of for far too long. The call to follow Jesus isn't a call to add Jesus as an accessory onto our lives. It's a call to become something new; to become whole; to forget our past loves; and to become like Jesus. But the only way we get there is through the costly process of dying to ourselves, taking up our crosses, and following Jesus.

All this talk of following and surrender only sounds costly because of how much we love the things of the world above the things of God. We calculate the cost of following Jesus based on the value of the things we must give up. This is where I've struggled. This is where the rich young man struggled. Instead of focusing on the joy to come, we focus on the sorrow of leaving our earthly idols. But we have this completely backward. The real cost is the other way around. The cost of keeping and gaining the world is losing your soul.

The gain of following Jesus is Jesus. The only one who can satisfy your soul.

What is your soul worth? Another home? Another vacation? A comfortable retirement? Food on the table? More entertainment? More leisure? Acceptance from those around you? Are you going to pursue the world at the cost of your soul or will you save your soul at the cost of the world? Will you set your focus on what you must lose to follow Jesus or will you adjust your focus on what you will gain by following him? All the world taken together for all time is not worth one single soul. In the end, the most costly thing possible is to gain the world at the expense of your soul. Let us not trifle with our souls. This is the call. This is the way of Jesus. Are you ready to follow? Are you ready to surrender?

This call may feel heavy and the way may look hard, just like it did for the rich young man, but once you lay down your life, you'll finally become free to follow in the way of Jesus. And on that road is grace, joy, and peace. On that road is rest.

CHAPTER THREE

LIFE OF SURRENDER

THE CALL TO follow Jesus leads to a life of surrender and submission. But what does this actually mean? How do we live this way? How do we move to the place where we see this type of life as the best life for us— here in this life and the next?

It begins with our hearts. It begins by gazing on Jesus and treasuring him above all else. As we do this, three predominant attitudes will overflow in our lives. These three attitudes are markers of a life surrendered to the way of Jesus.

FIRST ATTITUDE OF SURRENDER: KNOWING GOD IS BETTER THAN EVERYTHING ELSE

The first attitude is a confident belief that knowing God is infinitely better than what the world offers. Did you know that knowing Jesus is *the* ultimate promise that comes from following him? When Jesus invites us to follow him, he's inviting us to himself. As we follow Jesus, his infinite worth becomes clearer and deepens—and this cycle repeats the more we know the Lord. Soon we're pleading with God to give us more of himself, no matter the cost. This desire becomes the driving desire of our lives, but it all begins with following him.

Throughout Scripture, we see the promise that as we pursue knowing God, our strongest desire becomes more of him:

> *Delight yourself in the Lord, and he will give you the desires of your heart. (Ps. 37:4)*

> *If you abide in me, and my words abide in you, ask whatever you wish, and it will be done for you. (John 15:7)*

> *One thing have I asked of the Lord, that will I seek after: that I may dwell in the house of the Lord all the days of my life, to gaze upon the beauty of the Lord and to inquire in his temple. (Ps. 27:4)*

The first two verses are some of the most misused verses in the Bible. These aren't magic-genie verses we use to get whatever we want; they're statements about what we will want when we find delight in knowing God. What these verses say is that when we delight in knowing God—when we abide in him and his words—our desire for him grows. We want to know him more. When we want this and ask God for it, he'll give it. Always.

When we follow Jesus—by walking in his steps and resting in his words—we get whatever we want. It just so happens that what we want is more of him.

Jesus says, "Follow me and I will give you more of myself." That's it. That's the entire promise contained in the words, "Follow me." This is what the disciples got. They walked with Jesus for three years. They knew him. They abided in his teaching. In the end, they loved him so much that every one of them (other than John) gave their lives as martyrs for him. They were confident that knowing Jesus was infinitely better than anything the world offered, even their lives.

When Jesus bids us to come and follow him—to deny ourselves and lose our lives—the thing he promises is a deeper knowledge, love, and delight of himself. Will we be a people who say, "I want to know Christ no matter the cost"? To surrender to God and follow Jesus, we must come to a place where we believe that knowing God is infinitely better than everything the world offers. This is what the joyful man who sold everything for an eternal treasure knew. This is what the rich young man was offered but wasn't convinced was worth the cost.

To surrender is to say that knowing Christ is our ultimate desire. What is standing in between your soul and surrender? A follower of Jesus is intolerant of anything that might prevent him from knowing Christ more.

The first step is to renounce our sin and every idol we cling to and turn to Christ. Trust him to be our Savior, who took on our sin on the cross, absorbing God's wrath, and now opens a way for us to be reconciled to God. This is the gospel message. And then, as a saved people rescued by Jesus Christ, we follow in our Savior's steps, longing to grow in our knowledge of him. There is more to the Christian life—like pursuit of the spiritual disciplines and belonging to healthy, gospel-preaching churches—but not less than this.

Knowing God is *the* reward for following him. If we aren't spending time with him, how can we say we want to know him? That's absurd. If we want to know God, then our lives should be ordered around being with him. Let's be people willing to spend time with God so we can develop this first attitude of surrender as we come to know him more.

SECOND ATTITUDE OF SURRENDER: ABSOLUTE TRUST IN GOD

As you develop this first attitude of a surrendered life it will lead you to the second attitude—absolute trust in God. Knowing God more leads to trusting him more. It's that simple.

According to the dictionary, trust means an assured reliance on the character of someone.[1] In other words, when we trust someone we're confident that their character will produce every result they promise. When we surrender to God and start following him, what we're saying is we trust his character so implicitly that we'll follow him wherever he leads.

Without trust, we won't follow Jesus. Without trust in God's character, we'll never be able to say to him, "I'll follow you wherever you lead me. I'll go wherever you send me. I'll give whatever you ask of me." If the

1. "Trust." Merriam-Webster.com, accessed January 7, 2020. https://www.merriam-webster.com.

disciples didn't trust God's character, the story of the disciples would've ended soon after Jesus ascended to heaven. The disciples would've weighed the cost of following Jesus, licked their wounds, and gone back home. Instead, they demonstrated their trust in his character by continuing to follow and suffer for Jesus's sake. As a result, the world was changed.

So why is it hard for us to trust God? Why do so few of us take him at his word when he tells us that the only way to save our lives is to lose them? Why do we insist by the way we live that he is wrong about these things? Why do we respond in sorrow when we hear his call?

I'm familiar with this struggle. Near the end of 2011, my trust in God was put on trial. I had been working as an attorney for about seven years and was beginning to feel unsettled. I believed God was prodding me to use my legal training for something other than myself. At about that same time, I became aware of an international organization focused on ending slavery and human trafficking called International Justice Mission (IJM). As I learned about IJM, I concluded that this would be a great place for me to use my legal training to help others. So, I applied for a job and ended up getting an offer to work with IJM in Nairobi, Kenya.

As my wife and I prayed over whether or not to move our family of five to Africa (our boys were seven, five, and two), God confirmed that this was where we were supposed to be. It didn't seem as if we could go anywhere without people talking about human trafficking. We even sold our house without ever listing it. As my wife walked our kids to school one morning, she mentioned to a neighbor that we were thinking about selling our house. That neighbor just happened to be looking for a bigger home on our street. She and her husband came and looked at our house that afternoon and made an offer that night. It was as if God was saying, "Go."

As we began planning our move, I began to get fearful of the life that awaited us. Terrible traffic. Living an hour or more from work. My wife being homebound because of safety and carjacking concerns. My kids at a school more than an hour and a half from my work. A full day of travel away from our extended families—not to mention the exorbitant price tag. And on and on. So, after all of these plans, all of this confirmation, and selling our house, we backed out. We didn't go.

Very shortly after making this decision, my wife and I both felt very clearly that we had disobeyed God. Quite simply, he was leading us to go and we said, "No." When I asked myself why I had disobeyed, the answer became clear to me—I didn't trust God. I didn't trust he'd be enough for us as a family; that he would care for us, no matter what; that he would be with us as we followed him; that he'd give us more of himself amid the challenges. I simply didn't believe God was who he said he was and that the challenges were worth the reward of knowing him more.

Do you see why I said I'm just like the rich young man? I focused on the cost instead of the joy of the call.[2]

---

2. This event has served as the primary precipitating event leading us to pursue obedience even when it feels hard. From here we have learned much, as we have tried to say "yes" when we feel God leading.

I don't think I'm alone in this struggle. Even the famed nineteenth-century preacher Charles Spurgeon noticed it in his congregation:

> O unbelief, how strange a marvel thou art! We know not which most to wonder at, the faithfulness of God or the unbelief of his people. He keeps his promise a thousand times, and yet the next trial makes us doubt him. He never [fails]; he is never a dry well; he is never as a setting sun, a passing meteor, or a melting vapor; and yet we are as continually [troubled] with anxieties, molested with suspicions, and disturbed with fears, as if our God were the mirage of the desert.[3]

This is why we must know God to trust him. It's only in knowing his character that we can live in a manner that says, "God is a God who can be trusted." We trust him when we know him.

There are many great books on the character and attributes of God,[4] so I won't write at length about them here. Let me just point out a few attributes that cause us to trust him:

He is loving (1 John 4:7–8)

He is gracious (Ps. 145:8–9)

---

3. Charles H. Spurgeon, *Morning and Evening: Daily Readings* (London: Passmore & Alabaster, 1896), November 7.

4. A few books on the character and attributes of God: J. I. Packer, *Knowing God* (Downers Grove, IL: InterVarsity Press, 1973); A. W. Tozer, *Knowledge of the Holy* (San Francisco: HarperOne, 1978); Matthew Barrett, *None Greater: The Undomesticated Attributes of God* (Grand Rapids, MI: Baker Books, 2019).

He is merciful (Ps. 145:8–9)

He is just (Deut. 32:4)

He is good (Ps. 34:8)

He is faithful (2 Tim. 2:13)

He is wise (Rom. 11:13)

He is holy (Rev. 4:8)

He is unchanging (Mal. 3:6)

He is all powerful (Job 11:7–11)

He is infinite (Col. 1:17)

And, he is all knowing (Isa. 46:9–10).

All of these attributes converge at the cross of Calvary, where Jesus paid the ultimate price to reconcile sinners to himself. This is who God is. This is who is calling us to trust him as we follow.

When you trust the one you're following, your fear fades. Taking a step of faith becomes easier, even when you don't know how solid the ground is—not because you see the ground, but because you can see the leader. That's trust. If you don't trust the one you're following, you'll be skeptical and cautious, unwilling to take a step until you clearly see the ground. Instead of looking at the leader you're looking for the landing. Your eyes are on the wrong place. Surrender means you fully trust the one you're following. Trust that he is the only one who needs to know where your foot will land.

Jesus loves us so much that he laid down his life for us. With an infinite chasm between God and humanity due to our sin—and at an infinite price to bridge that divide—Jesus came in full humility to pay that price and reconcile us to himself. It's on this foundation that he calls us to follow him. This is a leader worth following. Will you trust that what he has in store for you is better than what you can see today? Will you take him at his word about where you find life? Are you ready to value everything in light of eternity?

Not one of us will ever stand before the throne of God, look in his face, think back to the things we "gave up" to follow him, and say, "I can't believe I gave those things up for you." Instead, we'll fall on our faces and worship him, longing for the chance to go back and trust him by laying it all down again and again to his glory. One thing is certain in eternity: there will be many who trusted God too little, but there will nobody who trusted him too much. You can't trust God too much. When we know God, we know this.

THIRD ATTITUDE OF SURRENDER: TOTAL DEPENDENCE ON GOD

This leads us to the final attitude that marks a life surrendered to the way of Jesus—total dependence on God. Once we know God, know his character, and believe we can trust him, we come to the point where we realize we can't do any of this on our own and must depend on God.

Dependence is a rather unpopular concept in our fiercely individualistic society. To be dependent is to be needy, weak, insufficient. To admit we can't write our own stories or be anything we want. Babies and old people are dependent, but not us. Independence is the thing every child craves and every aging adult desperately clings to. Dependence is a bad word in our culture. We'd rather be dead than dependent.

If you surrender your life to someone, however, you're making yourself dependent on them. If they take you down the wrong path, you're in trouble. When Jesus calls us to follow him, he's calling us to depend on him. To admit that left to our own devices, we can't succeed in anything—particularly in following him (Mark 10:27). This is the final attitude of surrender. This is where we lay it all down at his feet. Only from a position of total dependence can we deny ourselves, take up our crosses, and follow him.

Jesus constantly moved his followers to a place of dependence. They were as resistant as you and I would be—that is to say, they were vehemently opposed to it. My favorite example of Jesus doing this comes from John's Gospel. The night before Jesus is crucified, he spends intimate time with his disciples, comforting and teaching them. This teaching is known as the Farewell Discourse (John 14–17) and takes up nearly 20 percent of John's Gospel. At the end of this lengthy teaching, Jesus tells the disciples they can't understand what he's just told them, but if they wait a few days it'll all make sense.

Their response: "Now we get it" (my paraphrase of John 16:29–30).

At this, Jesus looks at them and tells them how they, in fact, don't get it and how they'll prove how little they get it by abandoning him in a few hours. Shortly after this, they all go to the garden of Gethsemane, the disciples fall asleep, Jesus is arrested, and the disciples flee. Their claims to self-sufficiency wither at the first sign of trouble. They didn't get it at all.

What I love about this story is the part I skipped. After Jesus finishes addressing his disciples and before going to the garden, Jesus prays for them. In this prayer, Jesus, knowing that the disciples are about to abandon him in his hour of greatest need, prays,

> *While I was with them, I kept them in your name,*
> *which you have given me. I have guarded them, and*
> not one of them has been lost *except the son of*
> *destruction, that the Scripture might be fulfilled.*
> (*John 17:12, emphasis mine*)

While knowing their deficiency of understanding and their impending failure, Jesus declares to the Father that he has not lost one of them—other than Judas. What an incredible declaration! He says that despite their deficiencies and failures he'll keep them. It isn't up to them getting it or staying by his side, it's his job to keep them. And he won't fail at his job. Don't miss this. Jesus is saying that it is his work that we must rely on, not our own. And he is working. He is always working. And he will keep those who are his. Our job is to depend on him and his work.

Jesus intentionally brought his disciples to a place of failure, where they would know that without God they could do nothing. They abandoned Jesus as he was falsely accused and convicted. They left him struggling under the weight of the cross; when he finally collapsed under its weight, a stranger picked it up instead of them. Then, they watched him die. Alone. I don't imagine they ever forgot the shame of abandoning their Savior in these moments. But Jesus had other plans. He knew that in order to keep them, as he declared to the Father that he would, they needed to become wholly dependent on him and the Holy Spirit. They needed to quit trying to do it on their own.

It was in this dependence—after Jesus rose from the dead and the Holy Spirit came to dwell in them—that they finally became effective.

And this is where Jesus is trying to take us. To the end of ourselves. He isn't trying to get us to do it better, he's trying to get us to depend on him. Hudson Taylor said it well, "God wants you to have something far better than riches and gold, and that is helpless dependence upon Him."[5]

How much self-reliance and self-trust do you exhibit in following Jesus? When you're working for God where do you begin? With a task list or on your knees? Do you think God needs your skillset, your financial portfolio, or your vision to accomplish his work? You're most effective for God when you're most dependent on God. Your greatest place of power is on your knees. In Matthew 9, Jesus tells his disciples that there is a large

---

5. Quote widely attributed to Hudson Taylor, though I couldn't locate the original source.

harvest (of people) and a shortage of laborers. Instead of telling them to go and labor in the harvest, he tells them to get on their knees and pray that God will provide laborers (Matt. 9:37–38). This is always the place we should begin—on our knees in total dependence on him. When we start here we become useful to the Lord.

This type of dependence requires humility. It requires giving up our rights to determine how a work will be accomplished. It requires a willingness to be led by someone else, possibly into difficult things. It requires remembering that this work is God's work and his alone. So, even as we follow Jesus, even as we obey his commands, even as we work out our own salvation, we know that whatever work we do through our power is nothing more than a filthy rag. But we still walk, we still obey, and we still work—not because it's beautiful and necessary, but because it brings God glory and delight as his children seek to know him, trust him, and depend on him.

When we try to do anything without depending on God, we make ourselves the hero. We draw glory to ourselves because it was our work. That isn't the heart of surrender. Surrender is acknowledging that God needs nothing from us and that we're the ones who need everything from him. It's focusing on God as the hero in the story. It's understanding that God's work doesn't depend on our ability. When we refuse to surrender to God by insisting that he needs our wealth, talent, or vision, we are living as if God's work is dependent on us in some way. Don't forget, this is the God who created a universe from nothing. He spoke and it came into being. I don't think he is depending on you or me for anything.

What if instead of looking at how we can be the hero in God's story, we prayed, "God use the weakest part of me for your glory. Humble me to bring glory to your name. Make it clear that it has nothing to do with me or my skill. Just let me know you more."

Dependence is taking up the yoke of Jesus and letting him lead (Matt. 11:28–30). It's admitting that the yoke of surrender is better than the yoke of self. We depend on God because his yoke of dependence is vastly superior to any yoke of works we fashion.

The call to follow Jesus is a call to surrender. When we accept this call, a few things happen. Our attitudes begin to change. Our knowledge of Jesus grows. Our love for Jesus flourishes. As these things happen, our ability to trust God blossoms. The lifestyle of trusting God we once looked at as radical or extreme now doesn't seem that farfetched—it may even seem normal. Our greatest longing becomes knowing God more, so we order everything around that. At some point, we realize that the best way to know God more is by following him more closely. Putting faith into practice and trusting God to do what he says he'll do and be who he says he is. So, we want to do that. We want to find ways to exercise this faith and trust. As we do, we wake up and realize that we're surrendering our lives to God. We're following Jesus. We're totally depending on God. We've quit looking to ourselves as the heroes. We've laid down our yoke and burden and picked up his yoke. We're no longer looking for our part in God's story, but God's glory in God's story. We want all glory to go to him and we live accordingly. For the first time, in our dependence and trust, we experience the freedom to follow Jesus wherever he leads. This is the way of surrender. This is the way of Jesus.

FIRST STEPS OF SURRENDER

Developing these three attitudes of surrender requires both belief and obedience. Following Jesus isn't just about believing the right things. Neither is following Jesus just about doing the right things. It includes both—believing and obeying.

Belief without Obedience

James, the brother of Jesus, tells us that if we believe the right things, but those beliefs don't move us to obedience, then our faith is worthless. It isn't really faith. He says,

> *What good is it, my brothers, if someone says he has faith but does not have works? Can that faith save him? If a brother or sister is poorly clothed and lacking in daily food, and one of you says to them, "Go in peace, be warmed and filled," without giving them the things needed for the body, what good is that? So also faith by itself, if it does not have works, is dead. (James 2:14–17)*

According to James, if we aren't following Jesus—as demonstrated by our surrendered obedience—it's evidence that we aren't saved. We don't know God. This doesn't mean we can be saved by what we do, but it does mean that if our claimed belief isn't coupled with surrendered obedience then we're demonstrating we don't know him at all. Our professed belief is worthless. No matter what we say we believe, we're not actual followers of Jesus.

It's ridiculous to claim you're following someone when you aren't following them. This is faith without obedience. Why claim to believe something you don't really believe? If you truly believe it, it would change you. Charles Spurgeon explains it like this:

> *We are not saved by serving Him, but we are saved to serve Him. From the moment we are saved, we ought to live in the service of our Lord. If we refuse to be His servants, we are not saved, for we evidently still remain the servants of self and the servants of Satan.*[6]

We aren't just looking to know *about* God, we're looking to know God. Knowing God only comes through belief *and* obedience. Knowing about God is very different from knowing God. The only way to know God is to follow him, which means we must walk as he walked. This is the only path of surrender.

Obedience without Belief

On the other hand, Jesus tells us that if we do the right things apart from faith and trust in him, then they're

---

6. Charles H. Spurgeon, *Following Christ: Losing Your Life for His Sake*, annotated and updated ed. (Abbotsford, WI: Aneko Press), 2, Kindle.

worthless. In one of the more terrifying passages of Scripture, Jesus says,

> *Not everyone who says to me, "Lord, Lord," will enter the kingdom of heaven, but the one who does the will of my Father who is in heaven. On that day many will say to me, "Lord, Lord, did we not prophesy in your name, and cast out demons in your name, and do many mighty works in your name?" And then will I declare to them, "I never knew you; depart from me, you workers of lawlessness."* (Matt. 7:21–23)

This is a passage that keeps me up at night. Look carefully at what this says: people are prophesying, casting out demons, and doing other mighty works in the name of Jesus and Jesus says, "I never knew you." Those are more works than most of us have ever done (or may even believe can still be done) and Jesus casts them out of his presence. What Jesus is saying is that just as faith without obedience is worthless so also is obedience without faith.

Sacrifice without surrender is a waste of time.

Not only is it a waste of time, but it spits in God's face. He isn't interested in ritual without repentance (cf. Ps. 51:16). He doesn't want us to give him our leftover worship. He's not looking for second place. He rebuked the Israelites for ritualistic worship time and time again in the Old Testament (see Isa. 1:11–17). He's not looking for actions without affections. He wants our deep and abiding love for who he is and what he has done. When we live a life of sacrifice without surrender we're telling God one of two things: (1) we can earn salvation or (2) we can use him to get what we want.

First, lives of sacrifice without surrender tell God we think we can earn salvation because of what we do instead of what he has done. We're saying by our lives that God must save us if we live a certain way and do certain things. Obedient surrender, however, arises from the belief that God has already done the greatest work in saving us. There is nothing more we can do. He has bought and paid for our salvation.

Trying to earn our way to God by our works inevitably leads to exhaustion and legalism. Exhaustion comes because it's impossible to be perfect no matter how hard we try. When we believe that our performance is what makes us right with God, we never know if we've done enough. Eventually we become exhausted and blame God for being a hard taskmaster. In response, we double-down and try harder. Increasing the list of rules we must follow as another attempt to improve our standing with God. In this mindset, we want to get to God through our efforts. This then leads to legalism. Ultimately, living this way makes us bitter, angry people who see nothing but law and obligation in walking with God. For most, this ends in resentment and rejection of God.

God never asks us to do anything to earn our salvation. Our obedience can't save us. We can't ever be good enough. We don't obey God to get to him. We obey God out of a response to his love for us and an understanding of grace. Only inside of that response, can we find life in obedience. God's call to obedience, his call to follow, is a call of grace. He is inviting us to walk in his path. The path of obedience. The path of Jesus. And this path is the only one that leads to life. Not because of our work. Not because of our steps. But because of his. This path leads us to peace and lasting joy. Not to exhaustion, rejection, or resentment. He is calling us to follow him on the narrow path that leads to life.

Take a look at his invitation:

> *Enter by the narrow gate. For the gate is wide and the way is easy that leads to destruction, and those who enter by it are many. For the gate is narrow and the way is hard that leads to life, and those who find it are few.* (Matt. 7:13–14)

The narrow way isn't easy ("the way is hard"). It's not the path commonly chosen ("those who find it are few"). But following on this path "leads to life." We don't choose this path because we can handle it on our own. We don't choose this path because everyone else is on it. We choose this path because of who is walking ahead of us. This is the way before us. It isn't promised to be easy, but it's promised to be good.

The second thing we tell God by living lives of sacrifice without surrender is that he's a tool we can use to get what we want—a divine vending machine. Whether it's for cultural or social standing or wanting something from God, the motivation centers on ourselves and not on God. We're all too willing to pretend as long as it benefits us, but as soon as it doesn't we're out. I believe this is what we're seeing in the West today. It has become socially and culturally acceptable to have no religion and, as a result, people are walking away from Christianity in droves. These are people who went to church and did church things not because they loved God, but because it benefited them. They had no faith or love or trust in God. Belief was convenient. Now that the rituals no longer benefit them, they're out.

Another type of person also tries to use God as a tool for their purposes, seeking to obligate God to bless or give them something based on their obedience. This is essentially the prosperity gospel today: if we press the right buttons, we'll get the results we want every time. What's the problem with that? It tells God that we can put him in our debt. That what he has already done isn't enough for our surrender and obedience. That when we obey, God owes us more.

A less overtly self-centered way people do this is by using the Bible as an instruction manual. The method here is to mine the Bible for secret codes or principles that lead to the "good" life. If we just do X, Y, and Z, then we'll succeed. Christianity is nothing more than a method for earthly success, a holy self-help manual. Now, don't misunderstand me, there are biblical principles that can lead to a rightly ordered life—just consider the book of Proverbs—but a rightly ordered life is the natural consequence of obedience, not its motivating factor. The Bible isn't our secret manual for comfort. When we follow biblical principles with an expectation that God will give us something in return, we're on dangerous ground. What happens when it doesn't turn out as we expected? What happens when we don't get the marriage we think we're owed? Or the kids? Or the promotion? Or the job? God isn't a genie. We can't take five steps and demand a result. That's not how obedience works. As Jesus promised, "In the world you will have tribulation" (John 16:33). We should look to God's Word for wisdom in how we ought to live, but never as a means to obligate God as if he owed us something. The purpose of the Bible is for us to know God, not to give us the six steps for an easy, successful worldly existence.

Trying to obligate God to give us something based on how we behave leads to bitterness and disenchantment. When the life we think we're owed doesn't materialize as we expected, a common reaction is to blame God. This attitude leads to bitterness because our "sacrifices" weren't appreciated and rewarded. Ultimately, many people who go through this discard their faith because God didn't work for them—in other words, he didn't give them what they thought they were owed. But God isn't a slot machine.

If we seek him for ourselves, we'll walk away with what we wanted—ourselves. Likewise, if we seek him for himself, we'll walk away with what we wanted—him.

Belief and Obedience

A life of following Jesus must include both belief and obedience. Belief is the thing that saves us—not the belief itself but the object of the belief, Jesus himself—and obedience is what provides assurance. I'm afraid we've determined that since obedience can't save us it doesn't matter at all. But nothing could be further from the Bible's witness. Obedience is an indispensable part of every follower's life. This doesn't mean we'll be perfect disciples, but it does mean we're on a new path of obedience, repenting of sin and obeying Christ. Faith without obedience isn't faith. If you say you're a follower of Jesus and have seen no change in your life, no obedience, no fruit, then that's a pretty good indication you don't know Jesus.

The other side of this coin is a bit tougher. It's possible that we'll perform acts that look like obedience without any belief. To see if this is present in your life, ask yourself what you desire most out of life. What do you hope to gain by following Jesus? Is it more of God? Or, is it something else? If it isn't more of God, then you need to take a hard look at why you are obeying. John helps us see the fruit of obedience and belief working together: "Whoever keeps [Jesus's] word, in him truly the love of God is perfected. By this we may know that we are in him: whoever says he abides in him ought to walk in the same way in which he walked" (1 John 2:5–6).

Following Jesus through both faith and obedience will radiate a love of God—which is what the apostle John means by "the love of God [being] perfected" in a Christian. When we follow Jesus, our love for God is perfected. This type of walk is present in every follower of Jesus, not just the "radical" ones. The previous verse adds, "Whoever says 'I know him' but does not keep his commandments is a liar" (1 John 2:4). In other words, if we say we know Jesus, we'll obey his commands and walk in the same way he walked. If we don't, we don't know him. This way of surrender isn't a call for a special few, it's the only call Jesus gives. We can't take a lesser call. This is the call to follow—the call he gives us.

The first steps of surrender begin with obedience, an obedience flowing from faith. These first steps might be tiny, but they will be steps. The thing we must keep in mind in this journey is that the way of Jesus is a way of growth and maturity. We don't start with the faith of the apostle Paul, Hudson Taylor, or George Müller, but we also don't stay at the faith of a new convert. We move and grow as our loves change. We increasingly become more like Jesus even as we at times feel like we're regressing. This movement that begins with faith, grows through obedience, and culminates in eternal life. Life in God's presence.

Are you ready to follow Jesus? To adopt the lifestyle of your Master? Are you ready to start walking on the path of Jesus? Are you ready to surrender your life? To embrace the call of the gospel? If so, let's begin by looking at the area of our lives that most of us, if we're honest, really don't want to surrender. Let's look at what the Bible tells us about following Jesus with our money and possessions.

BIBLE'S WITNESS OF FINANCIAL SURRENDER

"*WHEN IT COMES to money, all men are the same religion.*"

This critique was leveled at Christians by Voltaire in the first part of the eighteenth century. What he noticed was that Christians used and viewed money the same as everyone else. He could tell who claimed Christ by the beliefs they espoused and the things they opposed, but he certainly couldn't identify them by their use of money. As a matter of fact, he saw them bowing at the altar of money just like everyone else. Simply put, for the Christians Voltaire observed, money decisions had nothing to do with belief. Christians used their money no differently than anyone else.

Fast forward to today and this critique still rings true. If anything, it's even more on target. The pursuit of wealth has been codified as a moral good in our culture.

We celebrate wealth and material success above nearly everything else. The great tragedy in all of this is that many of our churches eagerly join in this celebration. The richest churches, pastors, and authors are lauded as our heroes and sages. We hold them up as models. We lionize the ones who can stand shoulder to shoulder with the elite of the world based on their wealth, position, and power.

As a result, there is a pervasive attitude of entitlement to wealth and comfort. After all, we worked hard for it. We should be able to do with it whatever we please. We know that as Christians we should care about those with significantly less than us, but not if it compromises our status or comfort. We'll help a little to make ourselves feel better, but not if it means sacrifice. It's all about our hearts anyway, right? As long as we help a little and care a lot, we can rest in the comforts of our wealth.

Is this the way it should be? Should Voltaire's criticism ring so true in our lives and in the lives of our churches? Is it okay if we look just like the world when it comes to money, wealth, and comfort? If not, how are we supposed to live? How do I even live differently from the world with my money? Who is living differently? Where are the examples?

If we look at the lives of Jesus, his disciples, Paul, the church in Acts, and the early church fathers, we see lives distinct from the culture, more concerned with proclaiming Christ than seeking comfort. When we look at the lives of martyrs and missionaries—Polycarp, Irenaeus, William Tyndale, John Bunyan, C. T. Studd, Hudson Taylor, Jim Elliot, and George Müller—we see lives distinct from the culture. In fact, their lives were so distinct that we still tell their stories, write their biographies, and esteem their faith. We revere them as heroes and champions of faith. We'll do anything it seems—except walk as they walked.[1]

Are we called to live like these people? Is this the way of Jesus? Or, are these merely figures to admire from afar? Heroes for sure, but not examples to follow.

What I want to explore in this chapter is what the Bible says about following in the way of Jesus when it comes to money. Is there a distinct way Christians are called to live with money and possessions? In other words, should Christians be demonstrably different than the world when it comes to viewing and using money?

APPROACH

Before looking at what the Bible says, I want to give an overview of how I approach the Bible.

First, on the personal side, I want to live a life formed by and conformed to the Bible. That is my starting point. This is my goal for you in applying this book to your life. While I'm not perfect in living this out nor perfect in my interpretation of the Bible, my goal is to get us to see the Bible's bigger picture. Whether you quibble with me or not, at the end of the day, you have to confront Jesus's teachings on money. He rebukes the

---

1. Paraphrase of Leonard Ravenhill, *Why Revival Tarries* (1959; repr., Bloomington: MN: Bethany House, 1987), 41. "We love the old saints, missionaries, martyrs, reformers: our Luthers, Bunyans, Wesleys, Asburys, etc. We will write their biographies, reverence their memories, frame their epitaphs, and build their cenotaphs. We will do anything except imitate them."

guy who builds bigger barns to store his crops (Luke 12:16–21). He warns against greed and covetousness (Luke 12:15). He warns about the love of money (Matt. 6:24). He warns that when we fail to care for each other we are not his people (Matt. 25:41–46). He warns that wealth makes it hard to enter the kingdom of heaven (Matt. 19:23–24). He instructs us to not lay up treasures on earth (Matt. 6:19–21). He instructs us to focus on eternity (Luke 12:32–33). He calls multiple people to sell everything and give it to the poor (Luke 12:32; Mark 10:17–22). He tells us to trust him for daily provision (Luke 12:22–23). He cares deeply for the poor and downcast (Matt. 5:3–12). He reserves his special promises for those without much (Luke 6:20–23). His teachings are hard, direct, and abundant. He didn't leave us in the dark on these things. We must hear what he says and then figure out how we respond as followers of Jesus. Jesus was over-the-top radical in his view of money. His words confront and challenge us. His words make us uncomfortable.

Second, on the interpretative side, I approach the Bible with the following three perspectives.

1. The purpose of the Bible is God's revelation of himself to us.

The Bible isn't a guide to worry or trouble-free living. It isn't a set of principles leading to an easy life. It is God's revelation to us of himself. The danger of using the Bible as an instruction manual instead of God's revelation of himself is that we'll almost always slide to picking and choosing the things we'll adopt and the things we'll ignore, taking verses out of context to fit our desires. This fails to recognize the nuance and complexity of God and his character and relegates him to a one-dimensional God who is afraid of the tension of reality. God places us in tension to draw us to himself. While we can and should look to the Bible for understanding how to live God-honoring lives, that isn't the Bible's primary purpose. Knowing God is.

2. When interpreting the Bible, I must look at the entire Bible and not just parts and pieces.

While the Bible was written by forty different authors over approximately 2,000 years, it presents one coherent and complete revelation. As I said, the Bible is God's revelation of himself to us. This revelation is only complete when understood through the whole Bible. As a result, if I want to get the whole picture of who God is, I must examine the whole Bible. I must never build a theology of anything off of one particular verse or passage. This means that in my interpretation I must understand the Old Testament in light of the New Testament and the New Testament in light of the Old Testament. I can't read either in isolation. When I approach the Bible like this I might have to weigh seemingly contradictory teachings on topics and allow these differences to inform my interpretation. This may mean that I don't fully understand God's revelation on a topic—and, since he's God and I'm not, this shouldn't surprise me—but what I must never do is disregard one teaching in favor of the other. I must engage with the tension and try to figure out, as best I can, how they each inform each other. This tension will ultimately drive me back to God as I ponder his complexity. When I interpret the Bible like this, I get a more complete picture of who God is, understanding the depth and breadth of his character, as I come to know him better.

Applying this approach to passages about money, what we see most often is that the New Testament clarifies and affirms the Old Testament. There is great synergy between the Old and New Testaments when it comes to passages on money. Almost every money principle from the Old Testament is carried forward in the New Testament. However, when we look at how the New Testament handles these principles, we realize that there were significant misunderstandings and misapplications of Old Testament passages that needed clarification. As a result, when interpreting any financial principle from the Old Testament, we must look to the New Testament to see what clarifications or apparent changes were made. Then we can interpret what is said. If the New Testament is silent on a financial issue, then our job is to examine the greater ethic presented throughout the Bible and ask how we can interpret the Old Testament principle in light of this greater ethic. The vast majority of abuses in teaching about money come from ignoring what the New Testament says about an Old Testament principle. If a New Testament teaching appears to be in direct conflict with one from the Old Testament, then we'd be foolish to ignore the New Testament teaching.

In summary, let's do the hard work of proper biblical interpretation.

3. When responding to the Bible's teaching, I must submit to the Bible and not make the Bible submit to me.

In other words, are we willing to let the truth from God's revelation of himself be reflected in the way we live? Will we conform our lives to the Bible or are we looking for the Bible to conform to us? When we come to the Bible in submission to God and his Word, we will leave changed every time. When we come to the Bible seeking justification for our lives, we leave unchanged, emboldened in our deceit, and hurtling headlong to a life separated from Jesus. The best way to submit our lives to the Bible is to study the life of Jesus and his followers and follow in their footsteps. When we do, we'll become more like Jesus and grow deeper in our knowledge of God.

Did you notice each of these three approaches to the Bible results in a deeper knowledge of God? That is after all the point of following someone—to know them. If you're reading the Bible faithfully and consistently with the right approach to God and his Word, then you'll end up with a deeper, more intimate knowledge of God. Following is all about being with someone. Getting to know them more. That is the point of all of this understanding and interpretation. It isn't about getting our best life now, but about knowing God more and pointing people to him by our lives.

On to the Bible.

OVERARCHING BIBLICAL THEMES ON MONEY

I once taught a seminary course called "Modeling and Teaching Personal Finance" as a one-week intensive for eight hours each day. It was indeed intense. Starting in Genesis, we walked through the Bible exploring what it said about money and possessions. As I prepared to teach and was teaching this class, I realized something profound. When given the opportunity to lay the truths of Scripture side-by-side in a condensed period of time, you can feel the weight of them. It becomes impossible to ignore their overall message. And what we saw were some painfully direct warnings about the dangers surrounding money. Certainly, there is nuance in how we each apply these truths, but without a doubt, the Bible warns that our view and use of money is a revealer of the condition of our souls. These aren't matters of preference or opinion. These are matters of faith. If we miss these things, we might end up gaining the whole world while losing our souls. We can't ignore these truths.

Here are five overarching biblical themes on money.[2]

1. Creation is a good gift to enjoy and steward for God's glory.

From Genesis, we see that God creates everything, looks at it, and declares it very good (Gen. 1:31). Then, in his generosity, he places all of creation under our dominion to steward for his glory:

And God blessed them. And God said to them, "Be fruitful and multiply and fill the earth and subdue it, and have dominion over the fish of the sea and

---

2. This list is by no means exhaustive; it's meant to be representative. Craig Blomberg's book *Neither Poverty nor Riches: A Biblical Theology of Possessions*, New Studies in Biblical Theology (Grand Rapids: IVP Academic, 2000) is a tremendous work on these topics. I commend it to you.

*over the birds of the heavens and over every living
thing that moves on the earth." (Gen. 1:28)*

God gives us the task of caring for his creation. This
is a significant and weighty task. As God's stewards,
we're given the responsibility of caring for the world.
We too often think of our stewardship as a responsibility only to our tiny speck of earth and only for
ourselves. But the task God gave is much grander than
that. It's a task to steward the whole earth and *every
living thing.* This means that our job is to care for more
than ourselves. While the primary sense of this phrase
in Hebrew refers to animals, it emphasizes we're to care
for all of God's created things. We have a responsibility
to each and every one of our fellow humans, over half
of whom are barely surviving. There is plenty of God's
good creation for everyone to enjoy, but only when we
stewards properly fulfill our roles.

If we truly love God's creation (including the people
made in his image) and want to enjoy it, then what
better way to do that than sharing our abundance
with others. Too often we behave as if the best way to
enjoy God's creation is to keep it for ourselves—as if
a life of comfort, luxury, and individual experiences
demonstrates proper stewardship and enjoyment of creation. This occurs when we ignore the broader call of
stewardship and dismiss the enjoyment found through
simplicity and sharing. Enjoying God's creation means
caring for it, not hoarding it.

One of the principal ways God leads us to enjoy
his good creation is through periodic celebration in

community. From the multitude of Old Testament festivals and celebrations to the seemingly wasteful displays of affection to Jesus in the Gospels (John 12:1–7; Luke 7:36–50), we see a God who wants us to celebrate him and his goodness. He told the Israelites to throw a huge party once a year with a tenth of their food and wine just to know him more (Deut. 14:23). God isn't a cosmic killjoy out to prevent us from enjoying his creation. He created good things and he calls us to enjoy them, especially in community with each other. Despite this invitation to enjoyment, this is far from a call to luxurious and excessive living. Each of these commands and examples is limited in both amount and frequency. They're exceptions to normal life—they're special, worshipful, and focused on God. God isn't calling us to live in continual lavish excessive celebration of ourselves. He is calling us to celebrate him and his goodness in community during periodic special times of worshipful celebration.

One key in properly enjoying God's creation is to enjoy it in tandem with our call to steward the earth. This means not thinking only of ourselves, and not treasuring the creation over the Creator. That means living lives of simple enjoyment both for our well-being and the well-being of others. Jesus tells us that this is the proper way to view and use creation—use it, but don't place your joy or hope in it. Don't get sucked into the trap of believing that a bunch of created things can bring lasting joy. Use them to celebrate the Creator, but never forget there is only one who can bring lasting joy. As Jesus reminds us,

*Do not lay up for yourselves treasures on earth, where
moth and rust destroy and where thieves break in and
steal, but lay up for yourselves treasures in heaven,
where neither moth nor rust destroys and where
thieves do not break in and steal. For where your
treasure is, there your heart will be also.* (Matt. 6:19–21)

Have you ever read this verse as a command? He
says, "*do not* lay up for yourselves treasures on earth"
(emphasis mine). He plainly forbids us from storing up
treasures on earth, just as he forbids countless other sins.
He knows any fortune spent or stored here is loss. You
can't hold on to it and you can't squeeze infinite joy out
of it, no matter how hard you try. Created possessions
will do you no good in eternity. God knows creation is
used best when it is used for the world and not simply
kept for or spent on ourselves. Moreover, when we use
it this way, we receive both present *and* eternal joy. As
stewards, then, our responsibility is to view and use our
possessions not based on what they can do for us in this
life but on what they'll do for us in eternity.

This is one of the greatest dangers in enjoying the
goodness of creation: that we'll come to prefer the gifts
over the Giver. This was the sin of Adam and Eve; one
we too must guard against. God gives us something
good and beautiful to enjoy, but when we worship it, it
destroys our lives and our relationship with God.

2. God will not be second (i.e., do not worship creation).
If we return to the story of creation, shortly after
God creates man and appoints him as the steward of

creation, man questions God's goodness, rejects his good plan, and chooses creation over the Creator. Man puts God in second place igniting a cosmic struggle that continuously strains to pull man's affections away from God. The consequences have been catastrophic.

God knows the struggle and its consequences and, therefore, commands us to put him first. In the Ten Commandments, the first two tell us to put nothing before God (Deut. 5:7–8). Moses tells the people of Israel that the point of the entire law is for Israel to "love the LORD your God with all your heart and with all your soul and with all your might" (Deut. 6:5). Jesus later affirms this as the most important commandment (Mark 12:28–31). What we see over and over in the Bible is that God will not settle for second place. He demands to be preeminent, not merely a part of our lives. When we put anything before God, we become separated from him, and following him becomes impossible.

While anything placed in front of God is destructive, money is singled out as being uniquely so. Jesus tells us,

> *No servant can serve two masters, for either he will hate the one and love the other, or he will be devoted to the one and despise the other. You cannot serve God and money.* (Luke 16:13)

Notice he doesn't say we shouldn't serve God and money—he says we *can't*. It's impossible. We'll love and serve one or the other. We can't serve both. Notice too what he says happens when we try to serve money and God: (1) you end up hating and despising God; and (2) devoted to and in love with money.

Pause and consider that. If you serve money in any capacity, you'll hate God. There is nothing neutral about it. Money is the only idol Jesus singles out this way. The only idol he says you can't serve it and him. Why? Because he knows how dangerous it is, how intoxicating its charms can be, and how easily we're seduced by its promises. When Satan tempted Jesus in the wilderness one of the three temptations he used was wealth (Matt. 4:8–10). Imagine trying to tempt the Creator of all things with more things. This means Satan believed wealth was powerful enough that it might entice Jesus to renounce his redemptive mission, not to mention commit idolatry.

And so Jesus singles it out and says you must choose: "Me or money. You can't have both."

The Bible, of course, doesn't prohibit us from having money, but it does warn us that money is chief among God's rivals. When we pursue or manage wealth, we're placing ourselves squarely within the crosshairs of God's chief rival. We're sentencing ourselves to the task of daily battling with the thing that can easily lead our hearts to hate our Father. Our command is to keep God first—to protect ourselves from worshipping the creation over the Creator. That means vigilantly pursuing all steps necessary to keep God first and money nowhere in the picture. If that means giving everything away, then praise God he'll meet us there. He'll take us from sorrowful obedience to joyful dependence on him.

God will not take second place.

3. Greed and covetousness destroy our relationship with God and are two of the chief means of turning our hearts from God.

Exploring the dangers of money a little further, we see two attitudes that turn our hearts from God: greed and covetousness.

These attitudes are warned against in the Ten Commandments twice as well, highlighting their importance. The tenth commandment is one we recognize addresses greed and covetousness: "You shall not covet ... anything that is your neighbor's" (Ex. 20:17). But greed is actually the focus of the eighth commandment as well: "You shall not steal" (Ex. 20:15). Clearly, taking someone's things is coveting—you wanted them so badly you steal. But this commandment is much more nuanced than that. This commandment has long been understood to encompass much more than taking something that is somebody else's. It actually includes keeping from others what we have the ability to share with them.[3] This means that when we have excess and keep more than our fair share, we're stealing from our neighbors who are barely surviving. This behavior is stealing every bit as walking into someone's home and taking their jewelry. The extra you have, God intended to be a blessing for your neighbor, not for yourself. This doesn't mean that you'll never have extra, but it does mean that you must prayerfully consider what is enough and what is excess and then seek to obediently distribute your excess to those who don't even have access to a basic standard of living.

---

3. Blomberg, *Neither Poverty nor Riches*, 40.

Further in the Old Testament, we see much of the law aimed at preventing abuses caused by greed. Two of the major aims of the law are protecting against abject poverty and limiting the over-accumulation of property. There is a perpetual movement toward fairness and equality in the law—it's unrelenting in its goal for everyone to have enough. As a result, those with more must help those with less. The law recognizes the reality that left unchecked our greed will lead us to disregard the needs of others, which ultimately leads to injustice and suffering. This doesn't honor God.

Next, the kings of Israel demonstrate ad nauseam what happens when greed runs unchecked. Greed is the precipitating reason the kingdom of Israel splits into two nations. Rehoboam, the son of Solomon—one the richest people who ever lived—wanted to be greater than his father. As a result, he increased Israel's burden and they rebelled, splitting the kingdom. Finally, after Israel's greed leads them deep into idolatry, God brings judgment on Israel and sends them into exile. If they can't receive the good that he has given them without worshipping it, he'll make it so that the only thing they have is him.

Then we move to the New Testament. If it wasn't already abundantly clear how much God hates greed and covetousness, Jesus, Paul, John, Peter, James and Jude all explicitly warn us to flee from it. Here is a sampling of biblical passages:

But God said to him, "Fool! This night your soul is required of you, and the things you have prepared, whose will they be?" So is the one who lays

up treasure for himself and is not rich toward God.
(Luke 12:20–21)

The cares of the world and the deceitfulness of riches
choke the word, and it proves unfruitful. (Matt. 13:22)

Put to death therefore what is earthly in you: sexual
immorality, impurity, passion, evil desire, and
covetousness, which is idolatry. On account of these
the wrath of God is coming. (Col. 3:55–56)

For you may be sure of this, that everyone who is
sexually immoral or impure, or who is covetous
(that is, an idolater), has no inheritance in the
kingdom of Christ and God. (Eph. 5:5)

The Bible lists covetousness in its hall of fame of
sins. It calls greedy people unfruitful fools who invite
God's wrath while flittering away their eternal inheritance. When I'm greedy, when I'm rich toward myself
and not toward God or others, when I believe more is
the answer, I'm providing evidence that I'm not following Jesus. And, as a result, when he calls me to follow
him, the call feels hard and I feel sorrow.

What's amazing about greed and covetousness is
that we seldom meet people who consider themselves
guilty of either one. This phenomenon led St. Francis of
Assisi to say, "Men have confessed to me every known
sin except the sin of covetousness."[4] Not only do we not
see this sin present in our lives, but we're also reluctant
to see it in anyone else's. It's as if there's this protective

---

4. As quoted in J. Vernon McGee, *Thru the Bible*, vol. 4 (Nashville:
Thomas Nelson, 1997), 301.

shield around any display of greed around our lives, especially in the affluent West.

This is preposterous. If you saw someone in your church struggling with pornography, you'd lovingly try to help them. You'd help them see the issue and gain freedom from the bondage of that sin. Identifying greed isn't about shaming people for the car they drive or the home they own, it's about coming alongside each other and wrestling together. It's about asking hard questions. Opening our financial lives to examination. Testing whether or not we've surrendered everything to God. Greed and covetousness are too dangerous for us not to be doing this. The stakes are too high. But for some reason, we've let this one go. This is a tragedy and it's destroying us. We have a greed epidemic. There's only one cure. Following in the way of Jesus unconditionally.

4. Wealth is dangerous, therefore be abundantly careful.

Are you starting to see a pattern? The warnings, testimonies, and dangers about idolatry and greed are overwhelming and they're everywhere. God didn't just give us an isolated warning, he littered the Bible with them. He gave us this massive red blinking sign and we look at it and pretend it's not there. It's as if we don't think God is serious about those things—that those warnings are for other people, but we can handle it. Money won't affect us the way it does others.

I have news for you: these warnings are for you. They're for all of us. We're not immune. God was serious. Let's take him seriously. Let's look at how the Bible portrays wealth and the wealthy.

Ecclesiastes tells us that wealth won't satisfy (Eccles. 5:10–15). Proverbs tells us that wealth is fleeting and won't last (Prov. 18:11; 23:4–5; 27:23–24). The prophets warn that the pursuit of riches and wealth will bring judgment on Israel; they lament that these two things are leading factors in the oppression of others and in injustice (Isa. 2:7–8; 31:7; Ezek. 16:49–52; 22:29; Mic. 2:1–3; Amos 5:11–12). Jesus tells us that riches choke out God's words and make us unfruitful (Matt. 13:22). He tells us that riches bring about worry, vanity, false security, oppression of the weak, and indifference to the needy (Matt. 6:25–34; 18:23–25; 25:31–46; Luke 10:29–37; 12:22–34; 14:17–21; 16:22–26). He says that riches make it hard to enter the kingdom of heaven (Matt. 19:23; Mark 10:17–31; Luke 18:18–30). James warns the rich to "weep and howl for the miseries that are coming" (James 5:1) because they "have lived … in luxury and in self-indulgence" (James 5:5). Revelation cautions that our riches make us blind to the reality of our souls and result in God spitting us out of his mouth (Rev. 3:14–22).

When we read all of these passages warning about money, it's strange how few take them seriously. We either ignore the warnings or believe we're spiritual enough to handle money—or simply conclude that it's not a big deal. If there were only one or two warnings I could perhaps understand this, but when we take into account the sheer number of warnings, it becomes inexplicable foolishness to ignore them.

As I taught through the Bible's witness on money in my seminary class, about six hours into our second day, it seemed as if the wind had been sucked out of the room. It was oddly quiet. Finally, a student somberly asked, "Was there anyone who handled wealth well in the Bible?"

Great question. You may be wondering the same thing.

The Bible's collective witness is that nearly everyone who had wealth was ruined by it. It almost always led to sin, idolatry, and forsaking God. There are a few positive examples we'll look at soon, but the truth remains that when you look at the whole Bible together you can't help but be overwhelmed by how often wealth destroyed a person's relationship with God; by how many people wealth kept from following God; by how much sin and idolatry it caused; by the wrath incurred on account thereof.

The warnings are clear. Wealth is dangerous.

Yet, there isn't a universal call for every follower of Jesus to divest themselves of all they have. That may be a call for some, but not all. The Bible doesn't promote asceticism; poverty isn't the ideal. Some may be called to voluntary poverty, but all are called out of involuntary poverty. Much of the Old Testament law and the promise of the coming of the Messiah (Isa. 61:1–2; Luke 4:18–19) were aimed at removing the conditions of involuntary extreme poverty from all people. We should never glamorize involuntary poverty as it's always oppressive and outside of God's good design for the world. That said, let's not fall prey to the opposite extreme and believe that God's design is for everyone to live in excessive wealth. Balance, simplicity, and nuance are key.

In studying the few positive examples of wealth in the Bible, we see two common themes emerge. First, they didn't pursue wealth as an end or even as a means to an end. As a matter of fact, nearly every one of the positive examples in the New Testament was already wealthy when they became a follower of Jesus. Anyone trying to use Jesus to gain wealth was swiftly condemned.[5] Second, they were generous. Every one of the examples in the New Testament was generous to such an extent that their generosity was recorded and commended. A few of the most prominent examples include:

Zacchaeus (Luke 19): A wealthy tax collector who after becoming a follower of Jesus gave away half of all he had to the poor and repaid everyone four times what he had stolen from them.

Joseph (Acts 4): A Levite who joined the first church in Jerusalem and promptly sold a field that belonged to him and gave it to the apostles.

Lydia (Acts 16): A merchant who after becoming a follower of Jesus opened her home for others to use.[6]

---

5. See Acts 8:9–24. Simon the Magician from whom we gained the word "simony"—in other words, trying to buy a position in the church.

6. Other positive examples in Old Testament include Abraham, who let Lot pick the land (Gen. 13); the Shunammite woman, who provided food for Elisha and made him a place to stay (2 Kings 4:8); David, Abraham, Joseph, Job, and Moses (all are relatively positive in how they handled wealth); Barzillai, who was generous to the king and didn't accept favor in return (2 Sam. 19:32). In the New Testament, we find Joseph of Arimathea, who was rich and used his wealth and position to give Jesus an honorable burial (Matt. 27:57); Dorcas, who was known for her charity (Acts 9:36); Cornelius, who as a centurion was known for fearing God, giving generously, and praying continually (Acts 10:1); Sergius Paulus, who was wealthy and then came to

According to New Testament scholar Craig Blomberg, "It goes too far to say that one cannot be rich and be a disciple of Jesus, but what never appears in the Gospels are well to do followers of Jesus who are not simultaneously generous in almsgiving and in divesting themselves of surplus wealth for the sake of those in need."[7]

Therefore, if you have wealth, beware of how dangerous it is and strive to live a life of extravagant, promiscuous generosity for God and his glory. Hold everything with a loose grip and an open hand. Look for opportunities to use the wealth that God has entrusted to you for his glory and his purposes. Live the life Paul exhorts followers of Jesus to live:

> *As for the rich in this present age, charge them not to be haughty, nor to set their hopes on the uncertainty of riches, but on God, who richly provides us with everything to enjoy. They are to do good, to be rich in good works, to be generous and ready to share, thus storing up treasure for themselves as a good foundation for the future, so that they may take hold of that which is truly life.* (1 Tim. 6:17–19)

---

faith (Acts 13:6–12); Jason, who used his home and resources to protect Paul and Silas (Acts 17:5–9); Aquila and Priscilla (Acts 18:2–3); Mnason of Cyprus, who willingly shared his home (Acts 21:16; nothing is said about his wealth other than that he had a house); Philemon, who probably had means since he had a slave and a house where the church met, though we aren't sure how wealthy he was; regardless, he shared his home and permitted the church to meet in his home (Philem. 1). This list isn't exhaustive, but it covers many of the positive (or at least neutral) examples of wealth in the Bible.

7. Blomberg, *Neither Poverty nor Riches*, 145.

5. How we use our wealth demonstrates what we believe and treasure.

This brings us to the final overarching biblical theme on money: how we use our money will tell us, and others, what we believe. When we become followers of Jesus the way we view and use money should dramatically change. If it doesn't, we need to ask what it is we believe and whom it is we follow.

The passages pointing to this final theme are some of the most challenging in the whole Bible. How we use our money can't save us, but it can reveal whether or not we're followers of Jesus. The Bible is clear that how we use or fail to use our money is a leading indicator whether or not we are following Jesus.

First, when I use my money to pursue the world, I demonstrate that I don't love God. As John exhorts,

> Do not love the world or the things in the world. If anyone loves the world, the love of the Father is not in him. For all that is in the world—the desires of the flesh and the desires of the eyes and pride of life—is not from the Father but is from the world. And the world is passing away along with its desires, but whoever does the will of God abides forever.
> (1 John 2:15–17)

Where is your treasure? In the world or in God? When money is spent pursuing the world, we demonstrate that the love of God is foreign to us. The love of God compels us to pursue people and relationships, not mere possessions and experiences.

Second, when I characteristically fail to use my money to care for the poor, I demonstrate I'm not a child of God. This is clear and it's terrifying. One of the first times we see this theme is from the prophet Ezekiel. Ezekiel is telling Israel that they're worse than Sodom—the same one God destroyed with fire from heaven because of their wicked rebellion. Do you know what Ezekiel says their prevailing sin was? "[Sodom] and her daughters had pride, excess of food, and prosperous ease, but did not aid the poor and needy" (Ezek. 16:49b). They had more than enough food and lived lives of prosperous ease and still didn't care for the poor, so God destroyed them. For the sins of indulgence and indifference.

The witness continues in the New Testament:

What good is it, my brothers, if someone says he has faith but does not have works? Can that faith save him? If a brother or sister is poorly clothed and lacking in daily food, and one of you says to them, "Go in peace, be warmed and filled," without giving them the things needed for the body, what good is that? So also faith by itself, if it does not have works, is dead. (James 2:17-17)

But if anyone has the world's goods and sees his brother in need, yet closes his heart against him, how does God's love abide in him? (1 John 3:17)

Both passages indicate that if we're people who can see a person in need and have the ability to help him, but refuse to do so, then we're demonstrating that we have no faith—that God's love doesn't abide in us. We quite simply don't believe what we claim to. For, if we did, we'd help those in need whenever it was within our ability to do so. Caring for the poor isn't optional—it's evidence of following Jesus.

Finally—and perhaps most terrifyingly—when I fail to use my money to care for my persecuted brothers and sisters in Christ, I reveal that God doesn't know me. According to Jesus,

> *Then [God] will say to those on his left, "Depart from me, you cursed, into the eternal fire prepared for the devil and his angels. For I was hungry and you gave me no food, I was thirsty and you gave me no drink, I was a stranger and you did not welcome me, naked and you did not clothe me, sick and in prison and you did not visit me."* (Matt. 25:41–43)

Nearly every commentator agrees that the people who weren't cared for in this passage were other followers of Jesus. This isn't a passage about how we treat every suffering person, it's a passage about how we treat suffering Christians. When we fail to care for our family of faith who are suffering, God will cast us out of his presence and into hell. Our neglect of our brothers and sisters betrays a lack of faith. When we can help and don't, we're revealing that we don't know Christ, not to mention a refusal to love Christ's church. How could we allow our brothers and sisters to suffer like this while we live so comfortably?

Friends, it matters how we use our money. While we can't spend our way to salvation, we can examine our spending and see the true condition of our heart. Let's not take these words lightly. Let's feel their weight and burden. Let's be grieved by what they reveal. And then let's ask, "What needs to change in our lives to follow Jesus with all that we are, including our money and possessions? What needs to change so we are ready to joyfully use everything we have to point towards God's glory in eternity?"

CHAPTER
FIVE

LIFESTYLES OF JESUS AND HIS EARLIEST FOLLOWERS

IF YOU'RE LIKE ME, you usually read the Bible in small bites, meaning reading a few verses or chapters a day. This is an excellent way o soak up God's Word, and I hope you do this regularly. One thing that this methodology misses, however, is the development of a singular theme throughout the Bible. As a result, it's easy to miss the weight given to some issues. In the previous chapter, I tried to overcome this shortfall by pulling together several passages on money. By themselves they're easier to skip, but taken together they stop you in your tracks.

Before we move on from the witness of Scripture, let's examine the lives of Jesus and his earliest followers. Jesus will show us what it means to walk as he walked. Jesus's followers will show us a group of people who were seeking to live out the lifestyle that Jesus himself had modeled. These examples will show us how we can apply the truths of who God is to the way we daily live as we strive to follow Jesus. As we look at this, let's remember Jesus's grace and compassion—the one who calls us to follow in his steps, but only after he led the way by dying in our place, absorbing God's wrath, and granting us eternal life. Let's remember that the one who calls is the one who loves and the one who leads.

JESUS'S LIFESTYLE

When God became flesh, he didn't do so as a member of the Jewish ruling society or as the son of an expert in the law. He came as the son of a carpenter from a tiny insignificant province under the control of the Roman Empire. Carpenters could make a decent living, and he likely had plenty of work in the Roman-controlled territory. We do know that his family was too poor to bring a lamb as a sacrifice at Mary's time of purification after Jesus's birth. Instead, they brought a single bird, which was only permitted if you couldn't afford a lamb (Lev. 12:6). The picture we get of Jesus is of an ordinary peasant. Poor, but not destitute.

We can presume that Jesus worked as a carpenter until he entered public ministry at around age thirty. At this time, Jesus gave up any comfort the life of a carpenter offered and adopted the lifestyle of an itinerant preacher—traveling around from place to place with no home. In his words, "Foxes have holes, and birds of the air have nests, but the Son of Man has nowhere to lay his head" (Matt. 8:20).

Jesus gave up his Galilean home to preach and minister. This wasn't the first time he had done this. When Jesus became flesh, he left behind his eternal home—the throne room of God in all its glory, might, and majesty. He had the entire universe at his feet and left it behind to be born to a young girl in an out-of-the-way town. As Paul says of Jesus, "though he was rich, yet for your sake he became poor" (2 Cor. 8:9a). Jesus became man for the purpose of wrapping himself with humanity and bearing it to the cross. He became poor and lowly so we might become spiritually rich. And we find these riches in a life following him.

As Jesus began his earthly ministry, he gave up even the simple comforts of his home. He walked away from his few possessions. As a traveling preacher who'd have to carry everything he needed, he traveled light, relying on others for shelter and provision.

Taking these things together, we see Jesus living a life with little, relying on others to care for him. His life's testimony was in laying everything down. Demonstrating an extravagant love for mankind as he humbled himself absolutely so we might know him completely. Making himself poor, so we might be spiritually rich. His love took him from the throne room of God to a manger and ultimately to a cross. This was the life of Jesus.

DISCIPLES' LIFESTYLE

Jesus's disciples came from a diverse background. While most were ordinary peasants (a safe assumption since approximately 80 percent of all people at that time were

peasants[1]), a few might've been relatively wealthy—
Judas, Levi (Matthew), James, and John as the most
likely candidates.

Regardless of their background, the disciples all
adopted the itinerant lifestyle of their Master. That
doesn't mean they all sold everything they had. Still,
we do know that while Jesus walked on earth, the disciples lived as he lived. They walked where he walked
and slept where he slept. They provided whatever they
could, but had abandoned the comforts of their lives
in pursuit of Jesus. After Christ's ascension, they continued living these abandoned lives, with all but John
dying the death of a martyr.[2]

EARLY CHURCH'S LIFESTYLE

With this picture of Jesus and his disciples in mind, let's
turn now to the example of the very first church—the
church in Acts. How did these people put into practice
their faith in Jesus? According to T. J. Bach, a missionary to Venezuela nearly a century ago, the "two distin-
guishing marks of the early church were: (1) poverty
and (2) power."[3] Not everyone was poor, but most were.
And this is how they lived:

> *And they devoted themselves to the apostles' teach-
> ing and the fellowship, to the breaking of bread and*

---

1. Blomberg, *Neither Poverty nor Riches*, 89.

2. Most Christian scholars hold that all of the disciples were martyred
other than John, who was exiled, and Judas, who killed himself.

3. Mark Struck, "World Christian Quotes," Desiring God, March 30, 2020,
http://cdn.desiringgod.org/pdf/articles/20110128_mission_quotes.pdf.

*the prayers. And awe came upon every soul, and
many wonders and signs were being done through
the apostles. And all who believed were together and
had all things in common. And they were selling
their possessions and belongings and distributing the
proceeds to all, as any had need. And day by day,
attending the temple together and breaking bread in
their homes, they received their food with glad and
generous hearts, praising God and having favor with
all the people. And the Lord added to their number
day by day those who were being saved.* (Acts 2:42–47)

Their fellowship included eagerly making their possessions available to other believers in need. And there were lots of needs. It was almost guaranteed that if you associated with Jesus at this time, you'd be kicked out of your home, excommunicated from your community, and fired from your job. The need was great which led them to worshipping God as they provided for each other, all while having favor with outsiders. And the church exploded.

I want to be clear that this wasn't an ancient form of communism. Even though there was a communal purse and nobody viewed their property as their own, there is no evidence that everyone divested themselves of all their private property. This was a voluntary extravagant sharing to meet needs as they arose among them. As a result, something astonishing happens: "there was not a needy person among them" (Acts 4:34a). These were poor, persecuted people. Yet, because of their generosity, nobody was in need. They had *eliminated* need in their community. Take a moment to consider the implications of that.

Another characteristic of the church in Acts was the extreme generosity of everyone with means. They sold fields, opened their homes, shared food, and people were drawn to Jesus. The lifestyles of these people were a powerful witness. As a result, the church grew. Paul's final words to the Ephesian elders perfectly sum up the overriding ethic of this early church: "It is more blessed to give than to receive" (Acts 20:35). These people were self-less givers, no matter how much or how little they had.

The three key markers of the early church were a dedication to God's Word, fellowship with one another, and extravagant sharing. This group of people followed Jesus with abandon. Their lives were compelling. This church drew people to God because of their distinct life-style. Imagine if we started living like this; if we cared for persecuted brothers and sisters this way; if we cared for the needy among us this way. What would happen? Would we eliminate need in the church? Is that possible? It happened once before. Let us not too quickly dismiss the way these people lived or the natural results.

PAUL'S LIFESTYLE

Through Paul's letters, we can piece together a good picture of his life. We know that he was born in a prominent Roman city to a Jewish father who was also a Roman citizen. This wasn't common for Jews, and it gave Paul significant rights that most Jews didn't have. As a result, he was a member of the upper-class Jews in Rome, studying under one of the most prominent rabbis of his day. He became a rising star as a Pharisee by zealously practicing his faith—so much so that he arrested and killed Christians. All of this makes up the following profile for Paul: upper class, highly educated, religious, and powerful.

Then, one day on his way to arrest Christians, Jesus appears to Paul and invites him to follow. This is a loaded invitation. If Paul agrees, it'll cost him everything. He'll lose his powerful position among the Jews. He'll lose his place among the Pharisees. He'll lose his status among the elite Jews of the day. And, most devastatingly, he'll lose his family. As if to make Paul's sacrifice in following that much more difficult, Jesus sends him to the despised Gentiles. This call to follow requires everything from Paul. He must lose everything that he previously treasured. He must walk away from his life.

And he does without hesitation.

After following Jesus faithfully for thirty years, Paul is in prison awaiting death. With time on his hands, he looks back over his life and considers all the things he gave up to follow Jesus:

> But whatever gain I had, I counted as loss for the sake of Christ. Indeed, I count everything as loss because of the surpassing worth of knowing Christ Jesus my Lord. For his sake I have suffered the loss of all things and count them as rubbish, in order that I may gain Christ. (Phil. 3:7–8)

He looks back at the things he abandoned to follow Jesus and calls them rubbish—literally, a half-eaten corpse and lumps of manure. What's even more remarkable about this statement is that Paul's life following Jesus wasn't filled with soft beds and dinner parties. As Paul recounts,

> *Five times I received at the hands of the Jews the forty lashes less one. Three times I was beaten with rods. Once I was stoned. Three times I was shipwrecked; a night and a day I was adrift at sea; on frequent journeys, in danger from rivers, danger from robbers, danger from my own people, danger from Gentiles, danger in the city, danger in the wilderness, danger at sea, danger from false brothers; in toil and hardship, through many a sleepless night, in hunger and thirst, often without food, in cold and exposure.* (2 Cor. 11:24–27)

Paul's life as a follower of Jesus cost him everything he cherished in this world. It led him to unimaginable hardship and suffering, ultimately costing him his life.

Paul could rejoice in his suffering and hardship because through it he came to know Christ. His life was consumed with his desperate pursuit of Jesus. There was no cost that Paul was unwilling to pay. He had weighed the options and knew his choice. No matter what challenge he faced, he knew he had chosen correctly. What seemed like a hard choice and an even harder life brought Paul joy, freedom, and an unrivaled intimacy with Christ. The way of Jesus was the way to life.

LIFESTYLES OF JESUS AND HIS EARLIEST FOLLOWERS

LIFESTYLE CONCLUSIONS

These lives are the best examples we have of how people nearest to Jesus tried to obey his call to follow him. How they were willing to follow him no matter the cost. These are the lives of people who knew that knowing Jesus is better than anything the world can offer.

So, what can we learn? What conclusions can we draw from these lives? Here are a few that stand out to me:

1. Following Jesus requires us to give up our former lives.

2. Taking care of the poor is non-negotiable.

3. Generosity is a characteristic of every follower of Jesus.

4. Following Jesus is worth losing everything.

5. If anything gets in the way of following Jesus, dispose of it immediately.

6. Material possessions ought to be held lightly and used promiscuously in pursuit of Jesus.

7. The pursuit of a follower's of Jesus's life is Jesus, not comfort or material wealth.

When we start seeing our lives as these people did, we move from trying to find the minimum require-ments for obedience to seeking maximum commitment to God's glory. We move from asking, "How much can I spare?" to "What's it going to take?"

These are people who knew what they were gain-ing by giving up their lives. Will we learn from their example? Will we follow in their footsteps? Will we follow in the way of Jesus?

MISUSES AND CONFUSION

Hopefully, I've convinced you that the Bible calls us to view money in a radically different way than the world. The Bible clearly and consistently exhorts us to not worship money. If these things are true, why aren't people talking about them or preaching on them more often? Or worse, why do we hear the opposite message about money taught so often by people claiming the name of Jesus?

I can come up with lots of theories on why we don't talk about money, but the main one is we don't want to change. We want to pursue the world like everyone else. We don't like this part of the Bible. We might say we're ashamed of it. We look at people with more than us and want what they have. We even think we're entitled to it. If we work hard, we deserve to enjoy the fruit of our labor. Isn't it our right? Isn't it only fair? And so this mentality leads us to find ways around the Bible's clear teaching. We pick and choose parts of the Bible that aren't so inconvenient and focus on those. We either ignore or over-spiritualize the warnings. Before we know it, we've so twisted Scripture we believe that amassing money and possessions is honoring to God and displays his glory. As if God is honored when we demonstrate our deep and abiding love for the world.

So, we gravitate to teachers and authors who tell us what we want to hear, who affirm us in our greed. We see that they use the Bible to support their teaching. And so, we convince ourselves they're right. Here's what makes this difficult: most of the teaching that is off in this area is only off by a few degrees. In other words, it sounds plausible; it appeals to our flesh and love for the world, and so we want it to be true. So, when someone appeals to this desire, we're quick to accept it. As a result, this abominable teaching flourishes.

Remember this, though: just because someone uses the Bible doesn't mean they're giving you the truth. Satan tempted Jesus using the Bible. He used God's words in order to tempt Jesus to sin. Jesus, however, knew his Father and he knew Scripture, so he could see how Satan was twisting the truth. Like Jesus, we must know God and the Bible and be alert for devilish appeals to our fleshly desires and misused Bible passages. Knowing that Satan will try to deceive us by wrapping our selfish desires under cleverly packaged Bible passages. As Søren Kierkegaard explains, "man in his natural condition is sick, he is in error, in an illusion, and therefore desires most of all to be deceived, so that he may be permitted not only to remain in error but to find himself thoroughly comfortable in his self-deceit."[4]

When we want something to be true, we're often willingly deceived. Aware of this dangerous tendency, let's look at three of the most common ways people abuse and misuse the Bible. If you see any of these

----

4. Søren Kierkegaard, *Attack upon Christendom*, trans. by Walter Lowrie (Princeton, NJ: Princeton University, 1968), 201.

misuses, you should deeply examine the teaching and test it against what you know of God and the Bible.

1. Single-verse theology.

I addressed this abuse previously. This is a real danger for each of us. Single verses contain marvelous truths, but we must be careful about drawing universal or theological conclusions from them, especially when in isolation from the rest of Scripture's witness. We must read each verse in light of the context of the surrounding verses and book where it's found. Ultimately, each verse is to be understood in light of the whole Bible. This skill develops over time as we become better students of Scripture.

The most commonly misused passages come out of the covenants and blessings of the Old Testament, the Proverbs, and the so-called reward passages of the New Testament. Most abuses either take promises for a specific covenantal community and try to apply them to individuals today or take spiritual promises and make them about material blessing. This twisting sadly minimizes God's promises. God has all kinds of beautiful blessings for his children and they're vastly superior to material things—like nearness to God, seeing his face, knowing him more, broad access to a family of brothers and sisters in Christ, and on and on. These things are the promised hundredfold return of the New Testament. What more do we want? We need to be wary of teachings that use these promises to justify the fulfillment of our worldly desires. We must ask what Scripture teaches us about what God wants most for us and how we think he can best accomplish that.

2. Downplaying the danger of money.

Downplaying the danger of money is more of an attitude than an outright abuse of the Bible. Quite simply, though, it's irresponsible to imply that money isn't dangerous. When people fall into this misuse with teaching on money they'll stress that money is an inanimate object, just a thing. It isn't evil unless we make it evil by loving it.

While I agree that money is a thing and isn't evil per se, I think the Bible clearly teaches that the things money represents are far from harmless. Money represents power, status, and independence. Jesus associated it with the spirit of mammon—the worship of wealth. Even though money is inanimate, Satan aggressively uses it to try to gain our love and draw us away from God. When we downplay the danger of money and pretend that it's just a thing, we allow it sneak in and get a foothold. Once it has a foothold, the love of money isn't far behind. We'd never say an attractive man or woman trying to seduce us isn't dangerous. While that attractive person can't make us do anything, they aren't neutral. They're actively trying to woo us. Satan uses money the same way. He uses it to woo us from God. We must be on guard when it comes to money.

3. Using the "good dad" argument as justification for our selfish desires.

The final common twisting of the Bible in the arena of money is an appeal to the "good dad" in the sky. This misuse of passages like Matthew 7:9–11 basically goes like this: "If I, as a good earthly parent, want my kids to be successful, healthy, and happy, then God, if he's a good father, would want the same for me." Therefore, since I want to spoil my kids, God must want to do the same for me. This is the ultimate appeal to our selfish desires.

The glaring problem with this theology is that it's based on the assumption that we, as finite beings, can determine what is good and how God should act. I believe that God loves us and wants what's best for us. I believe that he cares deeply for us and isn't seeking to harm us. But I also believe that God knows what I can never know. And with my limited knowledge, I have no way of knowing what is ultimately best for me and my family. Perhaps the suffering I'm going through is keeping my heart close to God or keeping me from abandoning my faith. Perhaps getting what I want on earth is the absolute worst thing that could happen to my relationship with God. I simply can't know what God knows.

I do know God loved Paul and the disciples and wanted the best for them. In love, God allowed Paul to suffer. In love, he let each of the disciples suffer martyrdom or exile. The thing I'm certain of is God is in control and working. Just because we can't see the end of his work doesn't mean it isn't good. God, in his infinite wisdom, will work differently than we would. Don't buy the argument that you're as good and wise of a father as the infinite, omniscient, omnipresent, immutable Creator of the universe.

As we move ahead, let us remember the great weight of Scripture and the great witnesses of those who have gone before us. They are our teachers and guides. Will we follow their lead?

THE GREAT BARRIER

WHY ARE SO FEW walking in the way of Jesus with their finances?

Why are Christians indistinguishable from the world when it comes to giving, saving, and spending?

Why are the stories we tell of radical faith and trusting God so old?

Why have famous preachers replaced faithful missionaries as our new faith heroes?

Why does the sorrowful response of the rich young man seem like the natural response to Jesus's call?

Why does this feel so hard?

The problem, I believe, is that we like our lives just as they are. We don't want to talk about all of this lifestyle and money stuff, because we don't want to change. We're comfortable. Content with our leisure and entertainment. Fearful of losing any of it.

Simply put, we love the world. Or at least the promises of the world.

This is *the* greatest barrier to following Jesus—a love for the world. And this is why any call to part with the world feels hard.

Not only do we love the world, but we also want more of it. Not content with what we have, we strive and work and pine after all the world has to offer. Ignoring the warning of Jesus, "For what does it profit a man if he gains the whole world and loses or forfeits himself" (Luke 9:25), we want both—this world and the next. Convincing ourselves that this is possible. That this pursuit is both good and holy. So we embrace the world. In our homes and churches, we cling to the world. As a result, denying ourselves and taking up our crosses to follow Jesus sounds like a miserable, sad existence. We can't imagine giving up even some of the world, much less living like Jesus and his earliest followers. And we grow increasingly in love with the world, driving ourselves further from Jesus while jealously clutching our things.

Do we really want to live as if the world is offering us something better than Jesus?

WHAT DOES IT MEAN TO LOVE THE WORLD?

In order to understand how we can see and overcome this great barrier between us and a life following Jesus, let's look at what it means to love the world.

First John 2 warns against loving the world:

Do not love the world or the things in the world. If anyone loves the world, the love of the Father is not in him. For all that is in the world—the desires of the

flesh and the desires of the eyes and pride of life—is
not from the Father but is from the world. And
the world is passing away along with its desires,
but whoever does the will of God abides forever.
(1 John 2:15–17)

If we love the world, we don't truly know God. Of
course, this doesn't say we should hate the world.[1] It
isn't telling us to hate the things of this earth that God
made for us to enjoy. Hate is not the opposite of love
here. That wouldn't make much sense in light of the rest
of the Bible. Remember in Genesis when God created
everything and called it "very good"? Even after the
fall, we're called to care for God's creation. Therefore,
hating the world and the people in it can't be what John
means by not loving the world. So what does he mean?

The idea here is that we're not to make the same
mistake that Adam and Eve did and worship creation
over the Creator. We're to hate Satan's distortion of
God's creation as he tries to steal our affections from
God and put them elsewhere. We're to run from the lie
that the world is as good as it gets and flee from the
temptation to pursue the world as a pathway to peace
and happiness. Simply put, don't love life more than the
source of life.

There are three particular temptations John high-
lights that lead us to love the world: (1) desires of the

---

1. For a thoughtful reflection on this topic, see Joe Rigney, *The Things of
Earth: Treasuring God by Enjoying His Gifts* (Wheaton, IL: Crossway, 2014);
idem, *Strangely Bright: Can You Love God and Enjoy This World?* (Wheaton,
IL: Crossway, 2020).

flesh, (2) desires of the eyes, and (3) the pride of life. First, the desires of the flesh are lusts for physical pleasures, such as comfort, ecstasy, and leisure. Second, the desires of the eyes are the lust for what we see—also known as greed and covetousness. Third, the pride of life is a pride in what we have or what we've achieved. Each of these temptations tries to satisfy us apart from God. The first two offer pleasure in the things we experience or possess and the third promises freedom through control. All of these are enticing, promising ultimate life here and now with no need for God, with no restrictions on our pursuit of fleshly pleasure. John warns that these temptations are always present as they seek to win our affections. If left unchecked, they'll overwhelm our desire for God and leave us churning in a world where our desires can never be satisfied. Interestingly, these are the same three temptations Satan used on Jesus: (1) satisfy your flesh with bread (desires of the flesh), (2) satisfy your eyes with the kingdoms of the world (desires of the eyes), and (3) satisfy your pride by demonstrating your power over angels (pride of life) (see Matt. 4:1–11). Satan wants us to satisfy our desires apart from God. But Jesus resisted these temptations and empowers us to do the same.

Notice the really insidious thing about each of these temptations—they're unquenchable. When we yield to our lust for physical pleasure, the satisfaction is brief and the lust returns more unrestrained. When we indulge our lust for what we see, the enjoyment is fleeting as we gaze on something else we want. When we reach our highest aspiration, we look up and realize there's another summit to climb, even greater than the one before. And so, like the demon who after being cast out brought back seven more demons (see Luke 11:24–26), our desires return with even more strength. Convincing us that the brief pleasure we felt before can be felt again, but this time it will last. It doesn't. Still, we keep trying. Engaging in an endless cycle that will leave us unsatisfied, exhausted, and disgusted. This is the love of the world. It promises everything, doling out tiny bits of pleasure to keep us coming back, but in the end it takes everything, including our souls.

WHAT HAPPENS WHEN WE LOVE THE WORLD?

James bluntly states,

> *You adulterous people! Do you not know that friendship with the world is enmity with God? Therefore whoever wishes to be a friend of the world makes himself an enemy of God.* (James 4:4)

Enemy? When we decide the ways of the world— the enticements and allurements of our flesh—are worthwhile pursuits, we're setting our hearts against God. Being a friend of the world means behaving as if the world's ways are better than God's. As if the world has life, desire, and satisfaction better figured out than God. As if leaving the broad path of the world to follow Jesus on the narrow path is somehow to be celebrated as sacrificial because it's such a sad, difficult life. In doing this, we declare ourselves friends with the world. We reveal our desire to find approval from the world instead of being willing to walk alone with Jesus. We can't have our eyes fixed on Jesus and the world simultaneously. Where we set our eyes is the direction we will travel. So, when we set our eyes on the world, we move toward the world. We walk away from God.

The scary thing about the love of the world is how sneaky and gradual it is. Nobody goes to sleep one night following Jesus and wakes up the next day pining after the world. It never feels that sudden. It always moves in degrees. Here is how I've seen the love of the world grow in people from a tiny seed to the rejection of God.

1. Friends and lovers of the world keep God at a distance.

They put up little walls and barriers to insulate themselves from God just in case they're wrong about him. Afraid to trust God and his promises, they hedge a little bit by letting the world have a place. What if God isn't real? What if Jesus isn't who he claimed to be? Scared of being wrong about God and missing the best of the world, they keep God at a distance and let a little more of the world in. And so the walls go up a little higher. The barriers become a little stronger. God is kept at a distance and the world is given soil to take root.

As this happens, the ability to take God at his word diminishes and the sway of the culture flourishes. They begin looking for acceptance from the world and become more concerned about what the world thinks than God. Obeying his commands and living in righteousness seems extreme and prudish. What would others think?

And this trend continues. The walls go higher.

2. Friends and lovers of the world develop an insatiable appetite for the world.

As the world gets more and more of a foothold, their desire for the world grows. Instead of defining happiness, joy, and success by God's standards, they redefine them by the world's standards. No longer do they strive for holiness, faithfulness, and obedience to God for these things; instead, they turn and look to status, wealth, and position.[2] Experiencing a little happiness, joy, and success in these worldly pursuits, they begin to convince themselves that if some felt good more will feel even better.

And so they dive headlong into the trappings of the world, sometimes claiming God's blessing. And just as the walls and barriers grow, so does this appetite. The more of the world they get, the more they want.

And this trend continues. The walls go higher.

3. Friends and lovers of the world quit wanting God.

Having walled off God and given the world free rein to root and flourish, friends and lovers of the world quit wanting God. The pleasures and promises of the world tempt them to believe that their best life is now. Eventually, God no longer holds any interest nor serves a real purpose. God might become something to be used, to fill their desires, but at this point the rejection is complete. The world has won and God is no longer needed or wanted.

---

2. Russell S. Woodbridge, "Prosperity Gospel Born in the USA," The Gospel Coalition, October 14, 2019, https://www.thegospelcoalition.org/article/prosperity-gospel-born-in-the-usa/.

This is the fate and the path of lovers of the world. This is the path to becoming an enemy of God. It starts subtly, but the end is always the same. When the world is given a place to take root, it always grows—just like a weed. And if we don't root it out, it'll spread and one day take over everything. This is how we become enemies of God. The problem is that a love for the world may not be obvious to us because it's so normal to our culture.

HOW DO I IDENTIFY A LOVE FOR THE WORLD?

If a love for the world is the greatest barrier to living a life following Jesus, then we must be able to identify this love in our own lives. The thoughts and customs of our age and culture effortlessly contend for a prominent position in our hearts. What I would like to do is raise some questions we can ask ourselves to help identify the areas where we are most prone to loving the world or where we actually are deeply in love with the world?

1. Are You Breathing?

In all seriousness, we need to admit that a love for the world resides inside us, therefore, we each need God's help. This is why Jesus said of the rich young man that with man this is impossible, but with God all things are possible. So instead of casting judgment on others who fail where we thrive, let's support each other in this battle.

2. Do You Look Like the World?

This is an especially tough one. What I mean is this: is your lifestyle distinguishable from most people in your life who don't know Jesus? Are there any differentiating marks in your lifestyle? I'm not talking about what you believe or even what you consider to be right and wrong. I'm talking about how you spend your money— what you eat, what you drive, how much you give away, how much you save, how you invest, etc. Has the world convinced you that its way with money is the best way?

We've convinced ourselves that living differently than the world is a unique calling reserved for a few— the ones with *special* faith. We're quick to point out that Jesus didn't call everyone to sell everything. The rest of us, we reason, are free to live like the world. What if we flipped this around by starting with the assumption that we're all called to commit everything to God's purposes? That our lifestyles shouldn't look exactly like the world's. Because when we live like the world—when we save and invest and spend no differently—we're saying with our lifestyles that we love the world. We may want a little Jesus thrown in to avoid hell, but we don't want to miss out on the world. In this mindset, Jesus becomes an add-on to a life in love with the world. And in the end, a life in love with the world has little use for Jesus.

When you look like the world, you can be sure you're on the broad path. You will not find Jesus there. The only thing a worldly lifestyle can do is distract us from the narrow path of Jesus. So why would we walk it?

3. What Dominates Your Mind and Time?

What do you spend most of your time pondering, desiring, mourning, and doing? The things we value most highly are the things we think about and passionately pursue. The things we have a low view of don't capture much of our thoughts or pursuits. What do the things we think about and spend time doing tell us that we most love? Paul tells us, "For those who live according to the flesh set their minds on the things of the flesh, but those who live according to the Spirit set their minds on the things of the Spirit" (Rom. 8:5). So according to Paul, whatever we set our mind to will determine what we pursue, which ultimately becomes the thing we love.

To discover what dominates your mind and time, consider these questions:

What is the easiest thing tfor me to talk about?

Do I spend more time pursuing and pondering God or my life and its pursuits?

Do I worry more about what the stock market did yesterday or the loss of tens of thousands of souls who died never having heard of Jesus?

Do I mourn more over the loss of a business opportunity or an opportunity to share the gospel?

Which of these things brings you to your knees before God? Ask yourself,

Am I content with a little when it comes to matters of the soul? Are you content with a little grace, with a little knowledge of God, with a little communion with God, with a little heavenly mindedness? But are you not eager for the things of the world, and never content and satisfied with what you have of them?[3]

---

3. William Greenhill, *Stop Loving the World* (Grand Rapids: Reformation Heritage, 2011), chap. 4, Kindle.

Let's not be people content to consume the bare minimum to survive in our faith as we gorge ourselves on the pursuits of the world. Jesus tells us, "Do not work for the food that perishes, but for the food that endures to eternal life, which the Son of Man will give to you. For on him God the Father has set his seal" (John 6:27). There's food and knowledge that passes away, and there's food and knowledge that doesn't. Consider which one you're pursuing. Does your pursuit say you love the world or God?

4. Are You Looking for the Line or the Lord?

Are you constantly wondering how close you can get to sin without sinning or looking for the minimum requirements to obey God? Are you looking for the line, inching up as close as you can? God isn't looking for speed-limit abiders. He's looking for surrender.

Jesus rebuked the Pharisees for living to the line and not looking for the Lord:

> Woe to you, scribes and Pharisees, hypocrites! For you clean the outside of the cup and the plate, but inside they are full of greed and self-indulgence. You blind Pharisee! First clean the inside of the cup and the plate, that the outside also may be clean. Woe to you, scribes and Pharisees, hypocrites! For you are like whitewashed tombs, which outwardly appear beautiful, but within are full of dead people's bones and all uncleanness. So you also outwardly appear righteous to others, but within you are full of hypocrisy and lawlessness. (Matt. 23:25–28)

The Pharisees focused on appearing holy. They identified the lines for obedience, and toed them. The problem was they weren't looking to obey God to know him more; they were looking to obey God to get more. They used God to gain the world—as if God was a divine vending machine dispensing goodies. And Jesus excoriates them.

Are you trying to get as close to sin or your Savior as possible? Are you trying to find the bare minimum to be acceptable to God, or are you desperately searching for ways to draw nearer to him? When your goal is nearness to God, you live differently.

One place I see this conversation about finding the line often is in the area of tithing. It seems as if most people who argue about tithing ask, "What's the minimum requirement that God wants from me? What's the least amount I have to give to get God's blessing?" This is just like the line-finding conversation in dating of how far is too far. But it's the wrong question. The question isn't how little I have to do, but what is the best way for me to know God more. What is the best way to honor God in this situation?

Sometimes we have to start with obedience with commands, but our goal should always be to move our hearts away from finding the line to finding the Lord. If we're constantly searching for lines, we'll miss the Lord. Our hearts will become like the Pharisees, and minimal moral obedience will become our means to gain the world.

5. How Concerned Are You about Maximizing Comfort and Minimizing Suffering?

Satan looks to buy our souls and he's willing to pay any price.[4] And I believe that he's found it for most people—in comfort and a quiet life.

First, he has convinced us that the pursuit of comfort ("just a *little* more") is harmless. It's nearly effortless for us to justify wanting a little more without feeling any guilt. After all, few of us think we live lavish lives, so we justify a little more comfort, when in reality that little more forever recedes in front of us until the day we die. Instead of longing for a little more comfort we should long for a lot more Jesus. One can satisfy while the other makes us hungrier. Don't let Satan buy you with the ever-receding promise of comfort.

Second, Satan has convinced us that a quiet life—one without suffering—is our right. He tells us that suffering and struggle are contrary to God's will. Yes, suffering is hard. It is endured, not enjoyed. God doesn't delight in our suffering. However, the Bible is clear that a life following Jesus leads to suffering:

> *Indeed, all who desire to live a godly life in Christ Jesus will be persecuted. (2 Tim. 3:12)*

> *... they returned to Lystra and to Iconium and to Antioch, strengthening the souls of the disciples, encouraging them to continue in the faith, and*

---

4. This is a paraphrase of a quote from John Rinehart made at the Kingdom Advisors conference in February 2019.

saying that through many tribulations we must enter the kingdom of God. (Acts 14:21b–22)

Remember the word that I said to you: "A servant is not greater than his master." If they persecuted me, they will also persecute you. (John 15:20a)

Beloved, do not be surprised at the fiery trial when it comes upon you to test you, as though something strange were happening to you. (1 Pet. 4:12)

Why would God tell those whom he calls that following him will lead to persecution, trial, and tribulation? What if God knows something about this road of suffering that we don't? What if it's actually in the middle of suffering where he is nearest, where we come to know him most intimately? If persecution, trial, and tribulation lead to those things, aren't they worth it?

In God's mysterious providence, I don't know why it works this way, but I do know we can trust the Lord and experience his tender mercies even amid suffering. Don't get me wrong, I'm seduced by comfort and a quiet life as much as anyone, but I want to desire more of God regardless of what comes with it. This is what Paul means when he says, "that I may know him [Christ] and the power of his resurrection, and may share his sufferings, becoming like him in his death" (Phil. 3:10). Paul knows that the path to knowing Jesus more is the path paved by Jesus, one of surrender and laying down our lives.

The way of the world looks easier, but it's a fountain of unquenched desire. The way of Jesus looks harder, but it's an ocean of joy and peace.

6. Do You View Following Jesus as a Sacrifice?

When you think about giving up your wealth or job or time or comfort to follow Jesus, do you look at these as enormous sacrifices? Should you receive honor for giving them up?

Remember Joseph of Arimathea? He was a secret follower of Jesus and a wealthy member of the Jewish council. He most likely sat on the council that condemned Jesus and sent him to Pilate watching silently, never revealing his love for Jesus. After Jesus's death, something unusual happens—Joseph becomes brave. He approaches Pilate and requests Jesus's body so he can give Jesus a proper burial. This act would've outed Joseph as a follower of Jesus, perhaps costing him his seat on the Jewish council and his standing in the community. Joseph potentially lost everything because of this selfless act of love.

So, here's the question: were the things that Joseph gave up for Jesus a sacrifice?

It depends.

If Jesus wasn't God, then what Joseph did was obscenely sacrificial. However, if Jesus was God, then Joseph received one of the greatest honors ever given to a human. He got to be a part of Jesus's passion narrative. This wasn't some sacrificial act for a good teacher. This was being chosen by God to care for the Savior in his greatest suffering and humiliation. And Joseph is still remembered for this generous act.

When we love the world, everything we give up can feel like an enormous sacrifice. We feel like the rich young man—sorrowful. However, when we see our "sacrifices" in the light of the cross and the empty tomb, everything changes. Nothing feels like a sacrifice. We can instead find joy in our obedience. To paraphrase missionary Jim Elliot, we're offering God that which we cannot keep in order to gain what we cannot lose. Joseph didn't do Jesus a favor by giving up his life. We don't do Jesus a favor by giving our lives for him. Jesus does us a favor by inviting us to follow him.

A proper view of Jesus, the cross, and eternity puts everything in perspective. It places us in a posture of joyful giving. It puts us at Jesus's feet.

Does this great barrier stand between you and Jesus? Do you love the world and the things of the world more than you love Jesus? Are you still unconvinced that a life following Jesus is better than anything the world can offer? That the call to lose your life is a call to joy and freedom? If you are, then the love of the world has taken root. This is a dangerous place to be. As James says, when we become friends with the world, we become God's enemies.

CHAPTER SEVEN

CHRISTIANIZATION OF THE GREAT BARRIER

MY MOM IS GOOD at knitting. She's so gifted that when I was a child, she'd knit me a sweater every year. These special sweaters were decorated with beautiful little yarn balls. (I'm pretty sure she added them to embarrass me.) Imagine the horror I felt each winter when I had to walk into school wearing my special new sweater that was clearly knitted by my mom—my bright red hair only made things worse. While I can appreciate my mom's love and care today, I hated the feeling of being exposed and vulnerable. I hated feeling like I stood out as the redheaded kid whose mom made his clothes.

I still don't like to stand out as different. Like most people, I prefer to fit in. This is another thing that makes fighting against a love of the world so hard. If we try to live without loving the world, then we're going to stand out. So we end up with a battle raging within us. We know we shouldn't love the world. We know it won't bring us lasting satisfaction or joy. But, we keep coming back looking for both acceptance and satisfaction.

One of the things that makes this an even harder battle is that many of our churches reinforce a love for the world in a variety of subtle and not-so-subtle ways. The places meant to guard us against loving the world are instead discipling us into a love for the world. We can't take the world, slap a Christian sticker on it, and somehow magically make it holy. No matter how we adorn it, underneath is still the same thing—the world—which leads us away from God. This practice of trying to Christianize the world has become ingrained in our churches, perhaps in imperceptible ways.

HOW THE CHURCH MAKES THIS HARDER

There is a popular management saying that says, "every system is perfectly designed to get the results it gets."[1] If that statement is correct and our churches are filled with consumer-minded, materialistic members, then there is only one logical conclusion: our churches, our practices, and the things we celebrate are perfectly designed to create consumer-minded, materialistic members who look no different than the world. If our church systems celebrate wealth, comfort, and entertainment, then what kind of disciples can we expect them to produce? These systems are often modeled after the "best the

---

1. Attributed to many, but most likely first said by Dr. Paul Batalden.

world has to offer" and can only produce a Christian-
ized version of the world.

This isn't a new phenomenon. The writers of the
New Testament warned of what happens when we let
a love of the world into our lives and churches. Charles
Spurgeon, in the nineteenth century, saw this same
phenomenon and commented,

> *I believe that one reason why the church of God
> at this present time has so little influence over the
> world is because the world has so much influence
> over the church.*[2]

> *Never were there good times when the church
> and the world were joined in marriage with one
> another.... The more the Church is distinct from
> the world in her acts and in her maxims, the more
> true is her testimony for Christ, and the more potent
> is her witness against sin.*[3]

When churches are built for convenience and entertainment, emphasizing the performances of preachers
and musicians, those criteria are what become central
to people choosing a church. We shouldn't, therefore, be
surprised when people demand that churches cater to
their preferences and needs. If they don't, they'll go find

2. Charles H. Spurgeon, *The Soul-Winner* (1895; repr., Lafayette, IN:
Sovereign Grace, 2001), 99.

3. Charles H. Spurgeon, "Separating the Precious from the Vile," Spurgeon
Gems, March 25, 1860, https://www.spurgeongems.org/sermon/chs305.
pdf., quoted in C. J. Mahaney, *Worldliness: Resisting the Seduction of a Fallen
World* (Wheaton, IL: Crossway, 2008), 23.

another church that will. A consumer-driven church
may attract a lot of people, but it's designed to produce
shallow, consumer-minded, entertainment-driven fans.
This type of church with the systems it deploys isn't
designed to produce faithful followers of Jesus. In fact,
they're better designed to lead people into a deeper love
of self and the world with a veneer of Jesus.

Just because a church has lots of people on Sundays
doesn't mean it's succeeding. What kind of disciples is
it producing? Lovers of the world or lovers of Jesus?
That should be the measure we use to identify thriving
churches. If the system we've allowed to arise isn't
producing faithful followers of Jesus, then it must be
replaced.[4]

IMPLIED PROSPERITY GOSPEL

I want to turn now to another danger lurking in the
church. It shows up in the words we use and the things
we celebrate. I call this the *implied* prosperity gospel. I
presume most people reading this book would outright
reject the prosperity gospel—the notion that God exists
to make us healthy and wealthy, which is ours to claim by

---

4. While the results of these consumeristic churches are tragic, they
have been written about quite extensively, so we won't dwell on them. See
Brett McCracken, *Uncomfortable: The Awkward and Essential Challenge
of Christian Community* (Wheaton, IL: Crossway, 2017); Erik Raymond,
"A Gospel-Centered Church Cannot be Consumer Driven," The Gospel
Coalition, February 29, 2016, https://www.thegospelcoalition.org/blogs/
erik-raymond/a-gospel-centered-church-cannot-be-consumer-driven/;   B.
Keith Haney, "Is the Church Making Disciples of Jesus or Consumer of
Ministry Services?" Christian Post, September 28, 2018, https://www.
christianpost.com/voices/is-the-church-making-disciples-of-jesus-or-
consumers-of-ministry-services.html.

having the right faith and/or doing the right actions.[5] The prosperity gospel is dangerous because it makes loving the world appear like a Christian virtue and promises the world as its reward, when in reality it's an exploitative system that preys on the weakest and poorest among us. In this system, God exists for our comfort and success. Lest we think we're immune to this erroneous theology, I suspect there are hints of this teaching in our lives and churches. Ask yourself these questions:

> *When you say that God has "blessed" a church or ministry, what kinds of things are you usually referring to? Financial success? Growth in numbers?*

> *When you think about "successful" churches or ministries, what kinds of metrics are you observing to make that determination? Number of members? Size of budget? Size of organization?*

> *When you think about increasing the "effectiveness" of your church or ministry, what do you measure? Attendance? Giving?*

I'd propose that just because our churches or ministries are big, financially successful, and growing doesn't mean God is blessing them. Consider Jesus's ministry. It seems that whenever the crowds following him get too big, he shocks them with his teaching. "Eat my flesh and drink my blood," he says on one occasion (John 6:53). Each time he does this, nearly everyone walks

---

5. See Costi Hinn, *God, Greed, and the (Prosperity) Gospel: How Truth Overwhelms a Life Built on Lies* (Grand Rapids: Zondervan, 2019).

away (v. 66). If you look at Jesus's ministry by numbers, he's a failure. By the end, there is barely anyone left.

The way we talk about God's blessing and success anchors it to the same treasures the world pursues. God's reality, though, is stunningly different. The blessings and successes of God's kingdom are inextricably interwoven with spiritual matters and realities. If God's promises were identical to those of the world, then God could be nothing more than a worldly creation; a god who could only give us the world and keep us from hell. A god like that is nothing more than the creation of a finite mind. A small, tidy god. A god impotent to fill our deepest longings. Our spiritual desperation. But our longings persist because God is omnipotent and he offers us infinitely more than the world ever could. He's made us to desire things that the world can never fulfill. And *these* blessings will satisfy our deepest longings in unimaginable ways.

Consider these questions:

When is the last time you thought of someone as being blessed who was undergoing suffering or persecution?

Do you consider Christians in North Korea blessed when they're arrested for their faith?

Do you consider missionaries in Buddhist countries successful who haven't seen a convert in five years?

Do you think God considers these people blessed and successful?

What spiritual realities does God see in the near-ness of these peoples' walks with him?

What blessings do they experience that you and I can't even fathom?

How do they know the deep soul satisfaction of God's presence in ways impossible for us to imagine?

I'm not saying God doesn't ever provide a church or a ministry with material resources or more people because of their faithfulness. I have no doubt he does. The problem is, we assume God's blessing when these things happen—so much so, that these have become the metrics we use in the West to gauge God's blessing in churches and ministries. Organizations now exist for the sole purpose of helping churches increase their mem-bership and giving. They come in and help churches implement "proven" strategies for growth—mimicking the "best" strategies from the business world. Why does any of that matter if lives aren't changed? Who cares how big your church or budget is if enemies of Christ sit in your pews?[6]

These "proven" strategies do nothing more than create a false sense of importance and success. If we aren't developing followers of Jesus, who cares about adding a few more consumers to our pews and turning them over to shake out a couple extra nickels. We need

---

6. For a helpful book on these ideas, see Gary G. Hoag, R. Scott Rodin, and Wesley K. Willmer, *The Choice: The Christ-Centered Pursuit of Kingdom Outcomes* (Winchester, VA: ECFA Press, 2014).

surrendered followers of Christ, not self-deceived cultural Christians.[7]

HOW DO WE VIEW MATERIAL GROWTH?

I believe God always provides the resources we need when we follow him. He tells us to first seek his kingdom and he'll care for our needs (Luke 12:31). Hudson Taylor famously said, "God's work done God's way, will never lack God's resources." I agree. I don't, however, think this means abundant resources are a sign of God's blessing. (Isn't this the same error Jesus corrected repeatedly?) God providing for our needs doesn't mean overflowing coffers of money. It may, instead, mean more stamina, endurance, or faith to persevere in the Christian life. This is where we're forced to enter the tension of life following God. We ask for his provision for the vision of his call, then we use whatever he gives. We maintain our focus on bringing God glory and inviting people into the richness of life following Jesus.

Material resources and growth aren't evils to be shunned in every circumstance. God periodically gives these things to his people throughout the Bible, particularly in the Old Testament tied to the covenant promises to Israel. However, material goods as rewards for godly living are unique to the Old Testament and always connected to covenantal promises for a specific group of people. We don't find these promises carried into the New Testament and we mustn't take them as

---

7. See Dean Inserra, *The Unsaved Christian: Reaching Cultural Christianity with the Gospel* (Chicago: Moody, 2019).

if they're meant for us.[8] Furthermore, we need to be careful that we don't take a description of something that was true in the Old Testament—for example, Abraham being "very rich in livestock, in silver, and in gold" (Gen. 13:2)—and believe it's a prescription for today.[9]

What we celebrate causes us to pursue and value those things. If what we value most is growing followers of Jesus by helping them know Jesus more, then whenever we experience material blessing or growth we'll look to return it to God's glory and use it to draw others into a knowledge of God. So, whenever there appears to be material blessing on a church or ministry, we need to ask why? Is this from God or is this Satan trying to draw us away from God? The material things and outward success are just as likely to be temptations from Satan as they are blessings from God. And even if they are from God, Satan will try to use them to draw us from God.

Let's be much more mindful of what we designate as God's blessing. God absolutely blesses his people. Following him changes our lives and satisfies our souls. We should celebrate these things and tell others about them. But, when all we ever celebrate are material things

---

8. Blomberg, *Neither Poverty nor Riches*, 84.

9. This would be the same as saying that polygamy is okay because many of the righteous people in the Old Testament lived this way. Descriptive parts of the Bible inform us of the way things are either specifically (historical books) or generally (wisdom books), and prescriptive parts of the Bible teach us how things should be ("You shall love the Lord your God with all your heart and with all your soul and with all your mind"). Confusing descriptive and prescriptive parts of the Bible leads to a lot of justification of lifestyle and wealth.

and worldly measures of success, what we're teaching ourselves and telling others is that Jesus is just another means to gain the world. As a result, we reinforce our love for the world.

BIBLICAL- AND NOBLE-SOUNDING JUSTIFICATIONS FOR LOVING THE WORLD

Before closing these two chapters on the great barrier to our pursuit of Jesus, I want to look at a few biblical- and noble-sounding justifications that are often no more than ruses for cultivating a love for the world. These are taught in some churches but are more often heard by people justifying their pursuit of the world and its comforts.

1. "It's my responsibility to provide."

As a father, I daily try to persuade my three boys of the importance of being responsible. I'm intent on teaching them to take good care of the things and relationships within their control and influence. While I'm all for people being responsible, the issue I'm concerned about is our proclivity of using "responsibility" as a justification for certain behavior.

What behavior?

I believe when we talk about being financially responsible as adults, we're almost always referring to providing for our families' current and future *physical* needs. The problem with this is that the Bible never places this responsibility on our shoulders. The Bible is clear that there is only one provider—God. We're commanded to care for our families (Deut. 6:4–5; Matt. 22:35–40; Mark 12:28–34; Luke 10:27) and diligently teach them God's ways (Deut. 6:6–7; 11:19; Prov. 22:6), but nowhere does God place the responsibility of provider on our shoulders.[10] That's his job.

Our call to care for our families is centrally found in the calls to love our neighbors as ourselves, honor our father and mother, and teach character and godliness to our children. Our responsibility is to share what we have, out of love, with our families and those with whom we are commanded to share, and to point others to God. This view of responsibility for Christ's followers emphasizes the spiritual needs of those in our care over other needs as well as the use of God's provision to care for physical needs of God's people, which includes our families.

---

10. Many cite 1 Tim. 5:8 as calling believers to provide for their family. I believe that this (1) takes this verse out of context and (2) misunderstands the connotation of the word commonly translated as "provide." First, 1 Tim. 5:3–16 is a section dealing with widows and the care of widows. Verse 8 is an admonition for people to care for widows to whom they're related. Essentially, it's saying that the first people who ought to care for these godly widows are their relatives and then, if the widows aren't cared for, the church should step in. Second, the word commonly translated "provide" carries the connotation of "thinking about" or "taking into consideration." In other words, in handling money, a relative must be open handed in considering widows and take them into consideration instead of clutching excess in self-indulgence. This verse isn't a call to provide for our children, our spouses, or ourselves. It's actually a call for our children to take care of us if we're widowed. Prov. 13:22 is another verse used to justify providing an abundance for our children. This is a complete misappropriation of the context and meaning of this verse. Because of the audience (not to mention the descriptive, not prescriptive, nature of wisdom literature), this verse could only be referring to a spiritual inheritance and godly character. Those things were the things that would permit the poorest of society to pass on an inheritance generationally and would protect their children from falling into the trap of dishonesty, debt, and slavery. See Thomas L. Constable, "Notes on Proverbs," n.p. Plano Bible Chapel, July 30, 2020, https://www.planobiblechapel.org/tcon/notes/html/ot/proverbs/proverbs.htm#head56.

When we assume the responsibility to be the provider for our families, we naturally become focused on physical provision for ourselves and our loved ones. This (1) puts us in the position that belongs solely to God and (2) disguises a love for the world. As a result, our "responsible" behavior ends up putting us in God's place and removing any need for us to trust God for anything. As providers, we come to believe that we must cover every contingency, insure against every loss, and plan for every disaster, justifying all of it by waving the flag of responsibility. We come to justify every expenditure, every indulgence, every gift, every self-indulgence as marks of a loving provider. These rationalizations permit us to disguise a love for the world as we "provide" for our families through every imaginable and excessive way. Where does this end?

Jesus commands us to not be anxious about the future and to trust him for our bare essentials, food and clothing. He took his disciples to the end of themselves in order to teach them it wasn't up to them. He was in control. He was the one who would provide. As we consider our call to care for our families and our desire to act responsibly, we can't usurp the command to trust God as our provider. We must consider how we develop that trust for ourselves and our families.

This is where our call to teach our children about God comes into full view. When looking at our families, consider what our actions say we're trying to provide. Freedom from having to trust God as their provider, or a life of faith trusting God as their provider? Are we focused on being a spiritual or physical provider? How much physical provision for ourselves or our family do we justify in the name of responsibility? How have we removed our need to trust God in the name of responsibility? I wonder if in heaven we'll discover that we trained our children not to trust God as their provider by trying to act as their provider. We'll have failed our call to train our children (spiritually) in the very act of trying to provide for them (physically). We'll have told them through our actions that we're their provider, not God.

The key distinction I'm trying to make is that God is the one who provides, and we're the ones who use that provision to care for our families and others, for both physical and spiritual needs. We must be careful with the words we use. God provides. We care and share. We must be careful never to use our call to care for our families as an excuse to remove the need for God, to spend and save with only our families' interests in mind, or to imbibe the natural desire for excessive self-indulgence.

One final thought. When we think about God's provision for us, we shouldn't immediately assume all of it is meant for ourselves. The Bible tells us that our material provision is given to help and benefit the body of Christ and the poor.[11] Why wouldn't God provide us with something to help someone else's need? Don't we have a responsibility to our *other* neighbors as well beyond our household? Is it only an emergency if it's happening to my own family? When did we come

---

11. Here's a sampling of passages on this topic: Lev. 19:9–10; 25:1–7; Deut. 24:19–22; Isa. 58:6–11; Ezek. 16:49–52; Amos 5:11–12; Mic. 6:6–8; Matt. 25:31–43; Luke 16:19–31; 2 Cor. 8–9; 8:14; Gal. 6:1–10; 1 Tim. 6:17–19; James 1:27, 2:14–19; 5:1–6.

to believe that we can justify neglect of the poor and persecuted in the name of responsibly supplying ourselves for decade upon decade? At what point have we become our own providers? At what point do we have enough? God tells us to trust him for tomorrow. He promises to provide our daily bread. Do we think his call for us to care for our families' physical needs goes significantly beyond this? Are we caring for ourselves and our unknown futures while neglecting others and their emergencies? These are all questions we need to be asking God as we seek to follow him. I can't tell you where the line is or how much is too much, but I can tell you that we should feel more tension between how we're called to care for our family and how we trust God to provide.[12]

Responsibility should never be used as a shield for the weightier things we're commanded to do or as an excuse to live however we want.

2. "I want to be able to be a big giver."

This one sounds noble, even biblical. You may also hear it this way, "I want to have a lot so that I can do a lot for God." Or, "I want to be rich so I can support a lot of God's work."

---

12. Some readers might feel unease in this section. Please don't misunderstand me. I'm not saying that God doesn't expect us to take care of our families with kindness and generosity, but I'm concerned with the language we use and the things we excuse in the name of responsibility, care, and provision. It's this last point that I'm trying to challenge in our thinking. Please don't think I'm telling you that you shouldn't take care of your family. I can't tell you what it means for you to care for your family, but I can challenge you to seek God's wisdom on what that means and then obey it.

There are a few glaring problems with these statements.

First, where is the focus? The giver who is the hero in this story, the one God "blesses" for the accomplishment of his work in the world. God needed him. Inherent in this statement is a desire for recognition. While the ability to give big gifts grows, so does the pride of being the one God uses to accomplish his work. This statement is all too often about being the hero.

Second, these statements assume that as a person's giving capacity grows so does their propensity for generosity. But studies have shown that this isn't true.[13] Wealth may lead to a person giving more actual dollars away, but it often leads to them giving less of a percentage of their income. The harsh reality is that the richer people get, the stingier they often become. The more they spend on themselves. This leads to the conclusion that the real reason most people want to become a big giver is the lifestyle accompanying that ability. The ability to gain more of the world. The giving ability is nice, but that lifestyle is even nicer. Being generous

13. According to IRS data, the most generous people based on percentage of income are those making $50,000 or less per year. There is a general downward trend in a percentage of giving for people from an income level of $50,000 to $2,000,000. Only above $2,000,000 does this trend reverse slightly, but people making over $2,000,000 per year still give less as a percentage of income than those making less than $50,000 per year. See, Matthew Frankel, "The Average American's Charitable Donations: How Do You Compare?," The Motley Fool, March 9, 2018, https://www.fool.com/retirement/2016/11/27/the-average-americans-charitable-donations-how-do.aspx. See also, Paul K. Piff, Michael W. Kraus, Stéphane Côté, Bonnie Hayden Cheng, and Dacher Keltner, "Having Less, Giving More: The Influence of Social Class on Prosocial Behavior," *Journal of Personality and Social Psychology*, 99.5 (2010): 771–84.

has nothing to do with the amount someone gives, it's determined by a heart of surrender. Generosity isn't a financial destination, it's a way of life.

Finally, these statements imply that God needs rich people for him to accomplish his purposes. Let me be absolutely clear here—God doesn't need anyone to be rich to accomplish anything. His kingdom isn't dependent on our net worth. He didn't need anything to feed Israel in the desert for forty years. Why do we think he needs our financial help? God doesn't have a money problem, he has a surrendered heart problem. Believing God needs our financial resources to accomplish his work is absurd. The reason that God's work done in God's way will never lack God's resources is that God is the one doing the work. He lacks nothing. He's not dependent on us to provide. God doesn't need more big givers, he desires more surrendered followers.

3. "We can't all give everything away."

Why not? Do we think if every follower of Jesus sold all of their possessions and gave them to the needy that we would die, starving and homeless, and Christianity would end in a generation? Or perhaps that there would be no one left to fund the work of the church? Honestly, what do you think would happen if every follower of Jesus, in obedience to his command, sold everything, gave it to the needy, and then trusted him to provide (Luke 12:33–34)?

I firmly believe that if we did this, we would see an outpouring of the Holy Spirit like nothing we can imagine. I believe the church would flourish and begin looking like the church in Acts. I believe that there would be enough for all of us—more than enough, in fact. Just like at the feedings of the 5,000 and the 4,000 (Matt. 14:13–21; Mark 6:31–44; 8:1–9; Luke 9:11–17; John 6:1–13). I believe God would faithfully fulfill his promise of food and clothing (Luke 12:22–32). He made that promise, didn't he? I don't think he'd be upset saying, "Oh great, I can't believe they thought I could take care of *all* of them. What will I do?" Of course not. He'd fulfill his promise.

Here's the other thing: giving everything away is just a moment in time. It's a moment of surrender. Tomorrow you'll have something. And you can give that away too if you want. This is more about a lifestyle and perspective change. It isn't about quitting working either. It's about being radically generous while continuing to work diligently, but working for eternal treasures instead of earthly ones. You really can give it all away. We're all called to surrender everything and be prepared to let it go on a moment's notice.

If you stop and consider this excuse for even a moment, you'll see how absurd it is. It displays a belief that we're more essential in providing for ourselves and the work of God than God is. I'll say it again, God doesn't need our money. He's looking for our hearts. Don't be afraid of this call. It may be for you. Are you willing to ask?

4. "As people who live under grace, guilt over possessions is unbiblical."

This is perhaps one of the brashest excuses for loving the world. It takes the grace of Jesus in his redemption and turns it into an excuse to live however we want. Since Christ's justification for sinners removes our guilt and condemnation from the law, Paul argues in Romans 6 that this freedom is never an excuse to indulge in sin.

While Satan often uses guilt against believers, the Bible is also clear that we aren't free to live however we want. We're told to not live showy lavish lifestyles (1 Tim. 2:8–10; 1 Pet. 3:3–4). Instead, we should thoughtfully examine where the line is between God-honoring joy in his provision and self-exalting luxury. Just because this is hard is no excuse for not trying. I have come to believe that there are lifestyles which are outside the bounds for followers of Jesus. Regardless of the freedom we have under grace, we must not damage our Christian witness through the exercise of that freedom (1 Cor. 9:19–23; 10:23–11:1).

There's another mentality at play here: as long as I'm doing some good things and believing the right things, I can do whatever I want with money. If someone challenges this setup, my defense is my actions and beliefs alongside God's grace. What's the glaring problem with that? It has nothing to do with grace. It uses my actions and beliefs to justify my lifestyle. It focuses on me and my works. In an effort to claim grace, I've jumped headlong into works as a means of justifying an excessive lifestyle at odds with the Bible. But I'm justifying a love for the world and the comforts of the world through a dangerous appeal to grace.

FINAL CAUTIONS

I fear I've stumbled on dangerous ground, giving stones to throw at affluent people in our churches. That isn't my intention. We need to give each other some leeway in this area, but we must stop pretending that any life-style is justifiable. Showy lavish lifestyles in a world of unspeakable poverty and lostness are a horrific blot on our witness.

Each of these four justifications are often nothing more than veiled excuses attempting to hold on to as much of the world as possible while trying to appear godly. When we do this, we're like the types of people Paul encourages us to avoid in the last days,

> *For people will be lovers of self, lovers of money, proud,…heartless,…lovers of pleasure rather than lovers of God, having the appearance of godliness, but denying its power. Avoid such people. (1 Tim. 3:2–5)*

Do we want to have the appearance of godliness but deny its power? Are we willing to use biblical sounding justifications to justify our lavish lifestyles and excessive accumulation of property? When we do this, we may still be able to look godly from the outside, but internally are falling deeper in love with the world. And as we've seen, falling in love with the world leads to becoming an enemy of God. These justifications must be carefully weighed, measured, and placed before God. If there is a hint of greed or love of the world in us or in them, we should quickly run the other way.

Loving the world is deeply ingrained in us; the world wants us to look like it (Rom. 12:2).[14] To love what it loves and celebrate what it celebrates. If we aren't aware of this pull and the danger it poses, we'll unwittingly wander onto the world's crowded road. As we look around and see so many people who look just like us, we'll assume we must be okay. With so many fellow pilgrims it becomes effortless to justify our lifestyles to hold onto as much of the world as possible. But we simply can't walk the world's road and end up with God. The world's road leads to the loss of our souls. There is no other destination. No matter how we try to justify walking the world's road, God isn't on it.

The only way to battle this love is to get off the road and follow Jesus. On the narrow path, we find the end for which we were created—being with God. Loving the world leads us away from God. We can't have both the world and God. We must die to the world. Only then will we be free to follow. Only then will we find life.

---

14. The word translated as "conformed" in the Rom. 12:2 is a passive verb that implies that the world is always passively trying to make us look and believe just like it. It'll try to conform our ways and beliefs to itself by the sheer weight and volume of the voices beckoning us.

WITNESS OF OUR MONEY

THE CONSEQUENCES OF loving the world are devastating for those who want to follow Jesus. We become devoid of God's love as we hurtle toward enmity with God. Not only that, when we display a love for the world by how we use our money, we simultaneously destroy our witness and malign God's name. Even if some disagree with my interpretation about the Bible's warnings against loving money, these other consequences should make us stop and consider what our lifestyles declare about our faith—and what that reveals to others about what we actually believe about God.

Not loving the world isn't about destroying everything we own and hiding in a cave on a deserted island. God has given us the charge to take care of his good creation. Therefore, not loving the world is more properly understood as stewarding the things of the world well by putting them in their proper places and using them for their proper purposes. All of which should point back to the glory and worth of God. Following Jesus is all about loving God and using things, not using God and loving things. This is what we're after when we try to not love the world.

Let's explore in this chapter how our use of money and possessions displays to a watching world what we believe about God.

REALITY OF OUR WORLD

Before we can understand what the use of our money and possessions communicates to others about our faith, we need to grasp the reality of the world in which we live.

1. Your standing in the world.

You're rich.

I hope that doesn't ruin your day or give you a big ego. Perhaps you've been reading this book thinking I was talking about someone else every time I mentioned rich people. I wasn't. I was talking about you.

Before you argue with me, let's review a few facts. Everyone who lives above the poverty line in the United States ($12,760 annual income in 2020)[1] is in the top 12.5 percent of the wealthiest people in the world. If you made more than $32,500 last year, you're in the top 1 percent of the wealthiest people in the world.[2] You won't

---

1. "Poverty Guidelines," Office of the Assistant Secretary for Planning and Evaluation, accessed January 30, 2020, https://aspe.hhs.gov/poverty-guidelines. This number is for an individual. For a family of four, the poverty line is $26,200.

2. Wealthiest ranking is taken from www.globalrichlist.com.

feel wealthy at these income levels, and I'm not trying to minimize the challenges that exist financially. In the U.S., it's difficult to live at the poverty line without getting some outside assistance. However, even in these difficult circumstances, you're considered wealthy compared to the vast majority of the world. The reasons go beyond just your income. They include your access to clean water, education, medical care, and a host of other services. All of these advantages put you in a category of affluence that few people experience or even imagine. By almost any measure, you'd be considered rich compared to the rest of the world. It's fairly astonishing once we realize how much more we have than the rest of the world and, yet, still don't think we have much.

We need to look up and change our standards for comparison. We're rich.

2. The spiritual and physical condition of the world.

There are over 7.7 billion people alive today.[3] Of this group, approximately 3.19 billion have never heard the gospel—these people are totally, completely unreached. Another 2 billion don't identify at all with Christianity. Of the remaining 2.51 billion people in the world, 1.74 billion of them are nominal adherents to Christianity and the rest (770 million) identify themselves as followers of Jesus.[4] That means that at best, between 10

---

3. "World Population Growth," Our World in Data, accessed January 30, 2020, https://ourworldindata.org/world-population-growth.

4. Joshua Project, accessed January 29, 2020, https://www.joshuaproject.net.

and 33 percent of the world's population are in right standing with God while the rest aren't. If these people die apart from Jesus, the Bible tells us that they'll suffer eternal separation from God (2 Thes. 1:5–10). Simply put, if the majority of the world never hears about or puts their faith in Jesus, their eternities will be horrific. With so many unreached and unsaved people, the spiritual need is overwhelming.

Not only is there tremendous spiritual need in the world, but there is also tremendous physical need. While great strides have been made in eliminating extreme poverty in our world, much of the world still lives in poverty. Approximately 10 percent of the world lives on less than $1.90 per day, and an additional 50 percent of the world lives on less than $10 per day.[5] That's 4.5 billion people living on less than $50 per week. Just as our affluence is experienced beyond our income levels, so is this poverty experienced beyond a lack of income. "The poorest in the world are often hungry, have much less access to education, regularly have no light at night, and suffer from much poorer health."[6] The effect of this systemic poverty leads to lower levels of education, higher incidents of disease, and premature death. Around 25,000 children die every day due to starvation or other preventable diseases directly related to poverty. To make matters worse, people in this type of poverty have no voice to cry for

5. "Extreme Poverty," Our World in Data, accessed April 21, 2020, https://ourworldindata.org/extreme-poverty.

6. "Extreme Poverty," Our World in Data, accessed April 16, 2020, https://ourworldindata.org/extreme-poverty.

help. It's as if their cries are swallowed by their misery, leaving them with no hope and allowing us to peacefully wallow in our affluence.

There is overwhelming physical need.

3. How American Christians are responding to the world.

Considering the relative wealth of Christians in the U.S. and the urgent spiritual and physical needs of the world, our response has been well short of inspirational. The average Christian in the U.S. is wealthier than 97 percent of the world, spending nearly 98 percent of their annual income on themselves—a piddling 2.5 percent of their income is given away. Only 2 percent of this giving goes to support missions of any kind. In other words, if you made $40,000 last year, you gave away $1,000 of it, with $20 going to missions. Out of this $20 to missions, just $0.40 supports mission work among unreached people groups.[7] That means the average Christian in the U.S. essentially finds a penny on the sidewalk each week and tosses it toward reaching the unreached. All while spending nearly everything else on themselves.

Based on mortality rates, around 65,000 people who have never heard the gospel die every day. And our response as the most affluent society that has perhaps ever existed is to throw a few pennies toward reaching these people each year. Does that make you want to vomit? Let's not even talk about actually going to work

7. Joshua Project, accessed January 29, 2020, https://www.joshuaproject. net.

as a missionary among these people. This is almost more depressing. Currently, there is one cross-cultural missionary for every 7 million people in the most isolated and unreached areas of the world.[8] That is a grand total of 277 missionaries trying to reach nearly 2 billion people.[9] That is staggering. I don't think I can overstate the need for missionaries to these people groups and yet so few are unwilling to go.

How can these things be true? How can we live in a world where we *know* of all of these unreached people, all of this poverty, all of this death, and believe that we have good news for them and do *nothing*? What does this say about what we believe?

WITNESS OF OUR MONEY

Jesus tells us that our hearts follow our money. In Matthew 6:21 he says, "For where your treasure is, there your heart will be also." In other words, the things we use money for will be the things we love the most.

What does our use of money say that our hearts love most? Comfort? Love? Security? Status? Family? Others? God? Does it say we love and trust God or does it say we love the world? When we don't respond to the urgent spiritual and physical needs of this world as we continue

---

8. Joshua Project, "Clarifying the Remaining Task," accessed January 30, 2020, https://joshuaproject.net/assets/media/handouts/clarifying-the-remaining-task.pdf.

9. Joshua Project, "Clarifying the Remaining Task," accessed January 30, 2020, https://joshuaproject.net/assets/media/handouts/clarifying-the-remaining-task.pdf.

to spend indistinguishably from the world, what does this communicate about the God we claim to follow?

Remember how Paul wrote that we become entirely new creations when we follow Jesus? He then says that as new creations we're "ambassadors for Christ, God making his appeal through us" (2 Cor. 5:20). As Christ's ambassadors, we represent the King and point others to him, including by how we use our money and spend our lives.

Do our actions and use of money make a compelling appeal about the worth of following Jesus? If not, what is their testimony?

Let's look at the testimonies we give to others when we use our money in ways that demonstrate (1) a lack of concern for those in spiritual and physical need, (2) a lack of trust in God, and (3) a lack of distinction in our pursuits with our money.

1. Lack of Concern

We explored two markers that demonstrate our lack of concern for those in urgent spiritual and physical need: an unwillingness to go tell them about Jesus and an unwillingness to use our resources to help relieve their spiritual and physical needs. Let's take each in turn.

First, when we fail to go and tell people the good news of the gospel, we're declaring with our inaction that we either don't care about the eternal state of others or we don't truly believe people need Jesus for salvation. If we actually believed that 65,000 people were dying every day having never heard the gospel and destined for hell, we'd do something. Doing nothing wouldn't be an option. I get that not everybody is called to become a cross-cultural missionary, but how many of us lose even a moment of sleep over all of these souls perishing without a chance to hear the gospel? Or as Leonard Ravenhill says,

> *Is life's span so dear and are home comforts so engrossing as to be purchased with my unfaithfulness and dry-eyed prayerlessness? At the final bar of God, shall the perishing millions accuse me of materialism coated with a few Scripture verses?*[10]

Sadly, we barely blink an eye when sacrificing for earthly pursuits. We'll move our families across the country, work long hours, miss important events, and sacrifice our marriages, all in the name of making more money and climbing the social ladder. Yet, we hear the call to go to dying, desperate souls and we respond without much thought, "I can't, it's too hard; it costs too much." What cost is it that we're referring to? The cost of our lives or comfort? What price is it that we're unwilling to pay for dying souls? The only logical conclusion the world makes is that either we don't believe or don't care. The world stands amazed at the impossible-to-reconcile inconsistency between what we say is the truth about people's need for God and our apparent lack of concern for telling people about him. Our lack of concern shouts to the world much more loudly than any of the words we speak. This has devastating consequences on our witness as followers of Jesus.

---

10. Ravenhill, *Why Revival Tarries*, 158.

Second, when we fail to sacrifice our resources to help relieve the urgent spiritual and physical needs around us, we're declaring that our comfort, future security, beauty, entertainment, to name a few common idols, are worth more than the physical and eternal spiritual needs of others. This unwillingness to give up much of anything for others shows that we don't take Jesus's words seriously. And perhaps don't believe them at all.

I know life isn't always this black and white. There may be times when we want to help, but don't see how. We might believe that there isn't any place in our life-style we can cut back. Or we might believe that what we have to offer, compared to the need, is like throwing a single drop of water on a raging forest fire. It won't change a thing.

This first excuse—an inability to cut back—is one of the great lies of wealth. Paul addresses this issue in his letters to the church in Corinth. This wealthy church had promised to help a poor church in Jerusalem, but they struggled to complete their promise. They had the same barrier exposed by this first excuse. Wealth. That may seem backward, but wealth is a huge barrier to cutting back. Why? Because as our wealth grows so does our anxiety about it diminishing. We convince ourselves that we live modestly and become anxious about any potential decrease in the lifestyles we've grown accustomed to. And the cycle churns contin-uously as our lifestyle creeps steadily higher and our giving remains unchanged.

Here's the problem with this: in trying to convince ourselves that we'd show our care through giving if we had more, we prove we don't care by failing to give up what we have now. Wealth traps us. It lets us grow accustomed to a lifestyle and then convinces us that anything less is a sacrifice too large. So, we buy the lie that we can't cut back to give. We demonstrate that we value our lifestyle more than the lives and souls of others all while assuring ourselves that if only we had more we'd give more.

The second excuse—that our giving doesn't make a difference—is a lie Satan spins. This belief that your drop of water can't make a difference is the lie that Jesus overcame in feeding the multitudes with just a few fish and loaves of bread. The amount we give in comparison to the problem isn't the key. The key is our surrender to God. God made the world from nothing; he can take your drop and turn it into a monsoon. It isn't your job to create the storm, just to sprinkle your droplet of water. We can't get overwhelmed with the need that is before us. While we can't fix everything—that was never our job in the first place—we can do our part and trust the Lord with the results.

There is one more common excuse for not helping those in urgent spiritual and physical need—it isn't our responsibility. This excuse stems from a belief that God wants us to enjoy our prosperity. After all, we'll always have the poor with us (Matt. 26:11). But it's clear from Scripture—as we saw in earlier chapters—that we're commanded to help our brothers and sisters in need and love our neighbors as ourselves, which includes those in spiritual and physical need. The story of the Good Samaritan shows us that being a good neighbor includes showing mercy at the cost of our safety, convenience, and well-being. To be a good neighbor means we're responsible to help when we know of needs. Furthermore, always having the poor with us doesn't mean we can ignore them. It means we'll always have the opportunity to display our care for others through generosity. We may periodically use wealth to celebrate God, but those are exceptions. In quoting Deuteronomy 15:11 ("For there will never cease to be poor in the land. Therefore I command you, 'You shall open wide your hand to your brother, to the needy and to the poor, in your land'"), Jesus's point isn't to encourage nihilistic withdrawal but sacrificial generosity.

When we behave with a lack of concern for those in urgent spiritual and physical need, the world notices. They are right to conclude that we are either cold-hearted or don't believe any of the things we proclaim. Doing nothing is not an option. Our faith demands a response and when we don't respond what other reasonable conclusion can people draw except that we are not the people of God.

But what happens when we use our money to help those with urgent spiritual and physical needs? We mustn't underestimate how powerful a witness this is.

In John 17, when Jesus prays for his disciples right before he's arrested, he prays for unity among them—a unity akin to the Trinitarian relationship among the Father, Son, and Holy Spirit. In fact, this unity amid diversity in the early church—Jews and Gentiles, men and women, rich and poor, all gathered together in the common worship of Jesus—produced such a generous church that *nobody* was needy (Acts 4:34). This unusual testimony of generosity produced a profound effect: they had "favor with all people" while the "Lord added to their number day by day" (Acts 2:47).

Paul's ministry also displayed an acute concern for the poor. One hallmark of his ministry was collecting offerings from one church to take to another church. He encouraged the churches to display their unity through generously providing for each other. This selfless generosity and care brought unity within the church and displayed curious charity to the watching world.

One of the greatest witnessing opportunities we have is in the way we take care of other followers of Jesus. Care that is so different people notice. I believe that if we gave as commanded in the Bible, we'd eliminate all needs in the global church. This isn't a pipe dream or communism, socialism, or any other -ism. This is simply what would happen if we took Jesus's words seriously by caring for our brothers and sisters in need. This is the hundredfold return that Jesus talks about in Mark's Gospel:

> Jesus said, "Truly, I say to you, there is no one who has left house or brothers or sisters or mother or father or children or lands, for my sake and for the gospel, who will not receive a hundredfold now in this time, houses and brothers and sisters and mothers and children and lands, with persecutions, and in the age to come eternal life." (Mark 10:29–30)

The hundredfold return is something we all receive when we follow Jesus and as we join the family of believers. Brothers and sisters ready to assist in times of need with community, shelter, and food. When we give as commanded, we become connected to each other in Christ's body so that there is no need among us. What's mine is yours and what's yours is mine. Don't underestimate the power of our unity shown through generosity. This witness will move mountains and bring the world face to face with the person of Jesus Christ.

We have a story to tell of the transformative work God has done in us and through us. That work should be on vivid display in our lives. People will notice. They will be confronted with who Jesus is. They will know they must choose. What glory this is! What fun this is! What joy this brings! So let's live lives that testify to our concern for the lives and souls of all of humankind.

2. Lack of Trust

Let's turn now and look at whether our lives, specifically how we spend our money, display a belief in the trustworthiness of God.

George Müller was known for his faith. He began an orphanage in Bristol, England, in 1836, determining never to ask for money. He'd petition only God. One of his three stated reasons for starting the orphanage was "that God may be glorified in so furnishing the means as to show that it is not a vain thing to trust in Him."[11]

---

11. Arthur T. Pierson, *George Müller of Bristol* (London: James Nisbet & Co., 1899), 123.

Through his life, Müller cared for more than 10,000 orphans and received over £1.5 million in donations and never asked for a penny. Every step of the way God provided. His life displayed that God is trustworthy.

If a complete stranger were to look at our lives and the way we use money, would they see a need for God? Would they say we trust God or a bank balance? Do we always provide ourselves a way out just in case God doesn't come through? As A. W. Tozer says,

> *The man of pseudo faith will fight for his verbal creed but refuse flatly to allow himself to get into a predicament where his future must depend on that creed being true. He always provides himself with secondary ways of escape so he will have a way out if the roof caves in. What we need very badly these days is a company of Christians who are prepared to trust God as completely now as they know they must do at the last day.*[12]

What does this life look like? We desperately need men and women unwilling to look like everyone else, unwilling to assume that what everyone else does is okay. Isn't the best place to learn faith and trust a place of absolute dependence? If we don't need God to come through, we don't have to trust him to do so. Until we become dependent on God alone, we're not truly free to follow him. I'm more convinced that we need people living in the middle of this culture trusting God for their today, not just for eternity—even when everyone else is

---

12. A. W. Tozer, *The Root of Righteousness* (1955; repr., Chicago: Moody, 2015), 58.

telling them not to put themselves in that position. The position of having to trust God.

We're in the middle of a generational walkout in our churches. Seemingly an entire generation of people are becoming adults and abandoning the church. I suspect one of the major reasons this is happening is because so few of us are modeling a life trusting God. People look around at the church and see a sea of people whose lives scream, "God isn't trustworthy. Take care of yourself." Or perhaps more accurately, "God isn't real." There is no trust, there is no power, there is no reality that marks our lives that anyone can point to and say, "I see a need for God there." When this is true of us, then why should our kids believe it either? What reason do they have to believe? If we spend our lives removing the need to rely on God, then we shouldn't be shocked when our kids don't rely on him at all.

We have the opportunity to use money—and our lives—in a way that shows to a desperate world that it isn't a vain thing to trust God. Sometimes you have to take the leap and say, "I trust you, God." Are you willing to stake your life on trusting him? Are you willing to say, "God, I love you more than things?" To say, "I'll manage my money in a way that honors you, not just in keeping my spending under control, but in how I use it. I will honor you with my wealth because you gave it to me to make your name known."

We must strive to make God's glory the aim of our lives. We should determine to use and dispose of our money in a way that shows that God can be trusted for today as completely as he can be trusted on the last day. This is the thing that will bring us the most joy and freedom. When we do this, it'll bring us more joy and freedom than we can ever imagine. And it'll display to the world that God is still—and will always be—the God who can be trusted. Stake your life on it.

3. Lack of Distinction

We already spent two chapters talking about not loving the world and the things of the world. I'll do my best not to belabor that point again, but I do want to explore what our love for the world proclaims about our beliefs about God.

"When the Christian church only cares about personal peace and affluence, which means I'm happy and I have enough for those I care about," observes Francis Schaeffer, "the church is fundamentally dead in the world."[13] When we live and pursue the same things as the world, it destroys our witness for Christ. What we're telling people is that Christ is just another means to get those things. But if this is the case, then Jesus becomes unnecessary and a burden. Once people realize this, they'll conclude they're better off pursuing the world on their own terms. Christianity offered this way—which isn't really biblical Christianity— will disappoint as it's nothing more than a pursuit of the world. This vision of Christianity is worthless. It

13. Jon Tyson, "Holy Ambition," January 13, 2020, New York City, Church of the City, Apple Podcasts, 41:25, https://podcasts.apple.com/us/podcast/church-nyc-holy-ambition-jon-tyson/id1245313998?i = 1000462408077.

proclaims that life with God offers nothing more than life without God.

We must turn these longings away from ourselves and point them to the only one who can satisfy, God himself. Until we do, we'll exhaust ourselves pursuing the world. Not realizing the reason we want this satisfaction is that God is calling us to himself, offering us what we can't gain on earth. Only an infinite God can satisfy our infinite desire. Our desires are far too frail and weak. When we pursue personal peace and affluence just like everyone else, we're telling the world that the God we worship can't satisfy their souls. We testify that this life is the best there is.

A lifestyle following Jesus testifies to our eternal desire. It challenges a materialistic culture and causes us to seek things far greater than personal peace and affluence. We're not trying to be different just to be different, but it says something about our beliefs when the world has no quarrel with how we live. This is a scandal to our faith. Our lives should tell a different story. They should point to the infinite worth of God. Instead of asking, "What is permissible?" let's start asking, "How will this affect my witness for Jesus?"

OUR OPPORTUNITY

We have an opportunity to show what we believe about God by how we use our money. When we use our money pursuing the world, the world is right to conclude that we don't truly believe the things we claim about God. If we did, our lives would look radically different. When we use money pursuing Jesus and making his name and glory known, the world will be forced to stop and seriously consider our claims. It may still dismiss us as delusional, but it can't condemn us as hypocrites or mercenaries. When we care for the poor and our brothers and sisters in persecution, our unity is our megaphone declaring God's worth with conviction.

All this glorifies God, which is the point of the entire thing. This isn't about doing more, but about following Jesus and living as he lived. If we want to follow Jesus, then we should behave as if we believe he's real. We should live as if we "are prepared to trust God as completely now as [we] know [we] must do at the last day."[14] As apprentices of Jesus longing to know him more, we get to know him more by living as he did. The more time we spend with Jesus and become like him, the more our lives will declare his goodness and trustworthiness. The more we feel joy instead of sorrow at the call to lay down our lives and follow him.

---

14. Tozer, *The Root of Righteousness*, 58.

CHAPTER
NINE

HOW THEN
WILL WE LIVE?

NOW WHAT?

We have this call to follow Jesus. To surrender our lives. Die to ourselves. Die to the world and the things of the world. This call, though, isn't a call to obey a list of rules and requirements to gain God's favor. It's so much more than that. It's a call to follow Jesus. To live a life modeled after Jesus's. This is a call to new life—to freedom and joy.

We also have this knowledge of the urgent needs in our world. We know that our response to these needs and the needs of our brothers and sisters either testifies to God's glory or brings derision to his name. We're appointed as ambassadors of Christ—his new creations—tasked with pointing people to the beauty of a life following him. So what do we do?

Too many of us desire to follow Jesus and sacrifice for those in need, but something holds us back. We look at the cost of following and it feels too high, especially when the return on investment seems distant and unreal. And so we wait. We feel sorrow at the difficulty of the call. Not really free to follow Jesus.

But we don't have to wait. We're free to follow Jesus today. On this path we aren't waiting for eternity to begin—we're seeking to do what Jesus did and walk as Jesus walked. Following Jesus is something we do today.

If all this discussion of dying to yourself and picking up your cross sounds exhausting, then I hope you realize that in calling us to die, Jesus calls us to live. As John Mark Comer writes,

> *We hear about his easy yoke and soul-deep rest and think, … yes, … yes, I need that. But then we're not willing to adopt his lifestyle. But in Jesus' case it is worth the cost. In fact, you get back far more than you give up. There's a cross, yes, a death, but it's followed by an empty tomb, a new portal to life. Because in the way of Jesus, death is always followed by resurrection.*[1]

Death is always followed by a resurrection in God's kingdom. This resurrected life of following Jesus leads us to know him more and become more like him. In dying we live.

It's time to take Jesus seriously in his call to follow him. This call isn't only for some Christians, it's for us all. Let's be honest, being stuck between two worlds is

1. John Mark Comer, *The Ruthless Elimination of Hurry: How to Stay Emotionally Healthy and Spiritually Alive in the Chaos of the Modern World* (Colorado Springs: WaterBrook, 2019), 83.

unbearable. Being lukewarm is a horrible way to live. Full of guilt for not doing enough, but not enough guilt to die to the world. Being stuck at wanting both God and the world, but unwilling to give up one for the other. I'd like to invite you to make a choice and accept Jesus's call. The call that will totally disrupt your life.

Let's look at three perspectives that will disrupt our lives. These are three perspectives that Jesus, the disciples, and nearly everyone who takes Jesus's call to follow seriously model in their lives.[2]

WORK DILIGENTLY

Lest we think the call to follow Jesus is a call to quit working, it's not. Jesus tells us to put down our yoke and pick his up, not lay down and nap. The call to follow Jesus is a call to work diligently in all we do. Work has been present and expected from the beginning. Genesis tells us, "The Lord God took the man and put him in the garden of Eden to work it and keep it" (Gen. 2:15). Man was created to work as a part of God's design for humanity.

The goodness of work is a theme seen throughout the Bible. Proverbs, in particular, is full of exhortations to the diligent and warnings to the lazy. Paul insists that our diligence in work is tied to our witness, giving his most direct teaching on this subject:

Now we command you, brothers, in the name of our Lord Jesus Christ, that you keep away from any

---

2. I have adapted these from similar observations I heard from Jimmy Seibert, David Platt, and William MacDonald.

*brother who is walking in idleness and not in accord
with the tradition that you received from us. For you
yourselves know how you ought to imitate us, because
we were not idle when we were with you, nor did we
eat anyone's bread without paying for it, but with toil
and labor we worked night and day, that we might
not be a burden to any of you. It was not because we
do not have that right, but to give you in ourselves an
example to imitate. For even when we were with you,
we would give you this command: If anyone is not
willing to work, let him not eat.* (2 Thes. 2:6–10)

As a body of believers committed to caring for one
another, we can only function properly when everyone
works hard within their unique gifts toward a common
purpose. If someone becomes unwilling to work and
expects the community to share with him, then Paul tells
us not to let him eat. Interestingly, this passage assumes
that the community is already sharing with each other as
the Bible commands. Why else would a lazy person need
to be cut off? Therefore, we work diligently so we don't
unduly burden the community with our needs. We work
diligently so we don't diminish our witness. We work
diligently so that the community is properly cared for.
We work diligently so as to make good use of the gifts
that God has given us. We work diligently so we have
something to share with the community (Eph. 4:28).

God gave us all different gifts and abilities, so work
will look different for everyone. The point is that whatever we do, we should do it diligently as worship to God
and as a witness to others.

Warnings on Work

Now that I've encouraged you to work diligently within your gifts, let me offer a few warnings.

Don't use the call to work diligently as an excuse to pursue riches. Working diligently in your gifting is biblical, but, as we've seen, seeking riches is dangerous. Be careful that the former doesn't become the latter. Don't convince yourself that your "gifting" is making money and, therefore, have divine approval to pursue wealth. Your gifting might naturally lead to some wealth, but there is a difference between pursuing your gifts to gain wealth and pursuing them to work with diligence for God's glory. How do we guard against having our pursuit of diligence turn into a pursuit of wealth? Make decisions ahead of time. Decide what limits you'll set on your life, what giving you'll do, how much you'll save, and what lifestyle caps you'll employ.

When considering how to use our gifts, the most important consideration is God's glory. The amount of wealth, power, or influence we can achieve, shouldn't cloud our decision. While it's easy to justify pursuing riches, influence, and power for God's glory, the inescapable reality is that when we pursue these things (no matter why) they almost always become our ultimate treasures. Before long we become so enamored with them, we compromise to protect them. Ultimately, they become the thing we refuse to part with to follow Jesus—they become first. This is catastrophic to our lives as followers of Jesus. God won't be second.

This, of course, doesn't mean Christians will never have wealth, power, or influence, but it does mean that when we do they won't be the coveted prize we've pursued. They won't mesmerize us with their seductive charms, preventing us from being willing to leave them for the One whom we are actually pursuing. Why? When we pursue Jesus, nothing else holds any deep value. This posture provides tremendous freedom to be unapologetic in our faith.

No matter how careful we are with wealth, power, and influence, we can't forget that these are the same things Satan used to tempt Jesus. They're powerful temptations. They'll devour us if we give them a chance. Let's not convince ourselves that God needs us to have these for him to use us.

Another thing that happens when we use diligent work as an excuse to maximize wealth is we end up driving behavior that can damage our witness. If our primary goal is making as much money as possible then we'll be wary of anything that will impede that goal. What if we prioritized people over profits by creating more opportunities for meaningful work? This may mean the owners make less money and the investors get lower returns. But each person will be treated as an image-bearer of God. What if we refused to work in certain industries or participate in certain business practices because they did not honor God? There are simply some jobs and activities that Christians shouldn't pursue. We are called to work, but that doesn't give us a license to do anything. Imagine what this would demonstrate to a world concerned with maximizing profits at any cost?

One final warning about working diligently. Don't let your work lead to entitlement, which is a peculiar cultural danger in the U.S. The idea that when we work hard we deserve the fruit of our labor is deeply ingrained in us; it's part of our American DNA. This makes it difficult to view our earned wealth as something that God provided and intended for his purposes. The Bible, though, is clear that God is the one who gives us the ability to work and earn money (Deut. 8:18; 1 Chron. 29:14; 1 Tim. 6:17–18). He's the one who equips us with the talents we have and puts us in the places he does so that we can earn the money we do. Let us not forget that the reason God calls us to work diligently isn't so we can get what we deserve, but so we can share with others as we live in community. Work is good because it leads me to generosity in community, not because it leads me to prosperity in isolation.

In Luke 5, when Peter sees the miraculous catch of fish, his response isn't, "I'm rich! Let's do it again." It's to fall down and worship Jesus, to put down his newly lucrative nets and follow. If we receive a windfall of success, our response should match Peter's. We should fall down and worship, and then get up and follow.

Is It Okay to Financially Prosper?

Before we move on to our second perspective, let me address one possible elephant in the room. Is it okay for us to be financially prosperous when pursuing our God-given gifts?

Short answer, yes.

The Bible has several examples of financially prosperous people following Jesus—Phoebe, Cornelius, Dorcas, and Philemon. The Bible doesn't prohibit business or making a profit, but it is emphatic in its warnings against making money an idol or hoarding it. The way to protect against these dangers is to avoid the temptation to let our business success be accompanied by an ever-increasing lifestyle or an ever-increasing stockpile. This is where we get in trouble. If we look at profit and success as something we deserve, we'll have a tendency to spend it on ourselves or sock it away for future possibilities. After all, we earned it. God doesn't give us wealth merely for our consumption. He gives it to us so we can display to the world that money is not our greatest treasure, Christ is.

Resist the temptation to assume that wealth gained is a blessing from God. Wealth can be as much of a burden as a blessing. It weighs us down and keeps us from running a light race. The price of wealth can be extreme. The time and mental energy needed to manage wealth often removes us from being productive for Christ. Don't seek to be burdened in this way, but if you are, use it to point to Christ and his worth.

To be clear, this isn't a call to asceticism. Neither wealth nor poverty is the end goal—surrender is. When we surrender and hunger for God, our longings change. What we want is more of God, to know him, to be in his presence, to give our lives to him. When we understand this and happen to have wealth, we're positioned to handle it well. We'll find ourselves giving great portions of it away, looking for ways to reduce our lifestyles, and humbly exemplifying a life of love (1 Cor. 13).

Our task is to work diligently for the Lord and use whatever gain results for his name and his glory. Our task isn't to enrich ourselves or live more comfortably. Our task is to walk in Jesus's footsteps.

LIVE SIMPLY

What sort of lifestyle does someone following Jesus embrace? In looking at Jesus's life, his early followers, and his most faithful followers throughout church history, one characteristic stands out—simplicity. The intentional removal of clutter and noise from life in order to more faithfully follow Jesus. Simplicity is what Paul has in mind when he writes, "[G]odliness with contentment is great gain, for we brought nothing into the world, and we cannot take anything out of the world. But if we have food and clothing, with these we will be content" (1 Tim. 6:6–8).

There it is. Simple living at its best—food and clothing. A life following Jesus leads us to godliness and contentment so we can be content with the basics. Because, ultimately, we find our contentment in Jesus.

This isn't about living sad lives, unwilling to enjoy God's gifts. Simplicity isn't even about changing an economic lifestyle, but rather about cultivating an attitude of joy and peace in God. Simplicity isn't a stopgap until we get to live lavishly, it's a lifestyle that frees us to follow wherever God leads. Enabling us to know God more intimately; removing countless distractions that prevent us from knowing God. This call to simple living isn't a call to sacrifice, it's a call to satisfaction. A call to know God more.

So what does it mean to live simply? First, let me say that I won't give hard and fast rules. This will look different for each of us based on many factors. The key in everything we've talked about in this book is to begin following Jesus. That means considering him and his will for the world in all we do. That means examining how we can use our money and possessions to know him more and join with him in his work in the world. Living simply is about liberating our hearts from the seduction of resources, freeing up more resources to pursue God.

As we approach any spending decision in the pursuit of simple living, a good question to ask is, "How does this help me know God more or join with him in his work?" Most of us don't think we spend lavishly or extravagantly, but this question helps highlight where we indulge without thought. There should be enjoyment of God's provision, but lavish celebration or comfort shouldn't be the rule of our lives. If we easily lavish ourselves and rarely say no so we can help others, then we've swung too far. As Paul says, "your abundance at the present time should supply their need, so that their abundance may supply your need, that there may be fairness" (2 Cor. 8:14). Our abundance has a purpose, and it's not increasing our lifestyle. It's to display fairness and unity.

Practically, this is hard. Living simply for God's glory isn't an easy transition to make. We can look at every spending decision and conclude that we could spend less. While that may be true, it isn't the point. The point is that most of us aren't looking at *any* spending decision and wondering if it's lavish or excessive. Since we're afraid to go down this path to its end, we don't venture onto it at all. Afraid of the slippery slope, we don't take a single step. We must deal with these tensions. We can't ignore the truth that few people are considering these questions at all. I say let's slip down this slope for a little while. Consider this example of the challenge presented by this shift in mindset.

In teaching these principles in a seminary class, I got a text message from my wife that many of the trees in our yard were diseased and needed treatment. These are big beautiful oak trees that frame our home and give it a lot of character. Losing them would be heartbreaking. Treating them, though, would cost $3,000. Was I willing to spend this much to save some trees on the grounds that it would help my home maintain its beauty (and value)? What else could we do with this money? Who else could we help? Would this bring God glory or join him in his work? We were struggling. A little later on the same day my wife texted me about receiving an inheritance of $10,000 from her grandmother's estate. Did that make spending the money on the trees easier since I now had some "extra" money? Was this God's way of providing for us to save these trees?

To be honest, I didn't have any good answers, but I was in turmoil. My gut reaction was to ignore the questions and spend the money. This wasn't a lavish expense. Some may say it would be poor stewardship to let those trees die. We prayed about it but didn't feel any clear direction. As we learned about the disease we realized that if we didn't treat our trees the disease would likely spread to our neighbors' trees, thus killing their trees or costing them lots of money for treatment. We decided to treat the trees, believing that harming our neighbor knowingly through our neglect didn't honor God. I'm not sure if we made the right decision, but I'm grateful we asked the questions. The important thing is to prayerfully ask the questions.

Once we decided about the trees, we had to determine what to do with the rest of my wife's inheritance. Should we give it away? Save for college? Pay off some of our mortgage? Paint our house? Replace windows? Save for a car for our teenager? There aren't easy answers, nor are my answers going to match yours. I could justify any of these expenditures. The key is considering how my usage of money is drawing me nearer to God and deeper into his work. I have to continuously circle back to my desire to live simply so that I may know God more and make his name known. My biggest mistake would be to assume that all I have is intended for my own "needs." When I make this mistake, I miss out on the contentment found only in God and the freedom of living simply.

Mindset of Simplicity

The biggest mindset shift we need is viewing our money like the church in Acts—not ours but available for those in need among Christ's body:

*Now the full number of those who believed were of
one heart and soul, and no one said that any of the
things that belonged to him was his own, but they
had everything in common. (Acts 4:32)*

Imagine if your church looked at possessions in this
way. What would change? What kind of lifestyle would
you adopt? How would this influence how you made
decisions?

A good analogy for this type of mindset is how
I spend money as a husband and father. Whenever I
want to buy something for myself, I consider the needs
of my wife and kids first. Do we have enough to cover
the things we need or have determined to spend on our
family? If there isn't enough, I don't buy the things I
want. I strive to live simply. As a result, most of my
spending benefits my family, and only periodically do I
buy things for myself. This is how we should view our
spending in light of the church. There may be wants
we get from time to time, there may be celebrations we
indulge in periodically, but as a general rule, we consider the needs of the church community prior to our
wants. Imagine if we all pursued living simply with this
mindset. What would happen? Would we remove all
needy persons in our midst as they did in Acts?

I want to be clear that living simply isn't just a call to
live frugally. Frugality is involved, but mere frugality is
nothing more than a miserly mindset that tries to pinch
and squeeze every penny out of every transaction. That
isn't healthy or God-honoring. Living simply may mean
buying a more expensive item because it's a better

long-term use of money or it supports local businesses or it doesn't exploit people in poverty. There are many reasons to not just look for the cheapest thing or the best deal. The mindset of living simply is a mindset of finding contentment in God above all other things, not merely how to spend less money. It focuses on knowing God and joining him in his work by making as many of our resources available to the God's work in the world.

We want to keep the money moving. Mere frugality often leads to hoarding, which is an insidious form of the love of money. This is a worship of money of a different sort. The point of living simply is to flee from becoming the clog in the drain with money. To let the money flow instead of engorging ourselves with it or stockpiling it to rot in our bigger barns.

Living simply is beautifully described in Proverbs 30:8–9:

> Give me neither poverty nor riches; feed me with the food that is needful for me, lest I be full and deny you and say, "Who is the Lord?" or lest I be poor and steal and profane the name of my God.

We take all sorts of Proverbs on their own and declare them as a model for our lives. Why not this one? This proverb beautifully matches the tension that so many of the Proverbs create between the goodness of enough and the dangers of excess. This verse sums up the life of a follower of Jesus. The desire is to know God most, and if poverty or riches make that difficult, then remove them from me. Let us, in our attempts to live simply, be people who desire to know God and make his name known above all other things. Let us seek the goodness of enough and flee from the allure of excess.

GIVE SACRIFICIALLY

It's entirely possible to work diligently and live simply without loving Jesus. Both perspectives, without the proper heart before the Lord, can lead us away from God, and into a love of the world—which is why this last perspective is imperative. It gives meaning to the first two and ensures they stay tied to the way of Jesus. Without intentionally and joyfully giving the resources we gain through diligent work and simple living, those perspectives become focused on ourselves and our efforts. Giving sacrificially is the engine that powers everything else. Without it our efforts are futile.

Giving sacrificially helps turn our hearts outward from our efforts and desire for control into the work of God in the world. It allows our lives to tangibly demonstrate that the things God calls us into are better than anything else. The physical act of generosity has a powerful way of forming our faith and deepening our understanding of who God is. It deepens our understanding of grace and eternity and permits us to tangibly display this understanding. A proper under-standing of grace leads to an overflow of gratitude for the undeserved forgiveness poured out at the cross. Grace, when properly understood, leads us to gener-osity. How else could we respond? Grace isn't a ticket to sin or live however we want. Grace is freedom from our selfishness. The clearest way to demonstrate this freedom is by giving sacrificially out of what we didn't deserve in the first place. We weren't given grace to fall back into selfishness.

A proper understanding of eternity—or, to say it another way, an eternal perspective—also leads us into sacrificial generosity. The anticipation of a far greater reality than what we are presently living changes the way we approach everything. Jesus tells us, "Do not work for the food that perishes, but for the food that endures to eternal life, which the Son of Man will give to you. For on him God the Father has set his seal" (John 6:27). What food will endure to eternal life? God, his glory, and the souls he saves. Therefore, if I want to work for this enduring food, I'll put my money toward those ends. I will give recklessly and sacrificially to glorify God and help lead people to a life of following Jesus. These are things that will endure to eternal life. Our view of eternity should massively disrupt the way we use money.

The struggle with maintaining an eternal perspective is that earthly treasures have the propensity to keep us from pursuing heavenly ones. The best way to deal with this propensity is to intentionally lift our eyes heavenward by investing in food that endures to eternal life. Setting our minds on storing up treasures in heaven instead of on earth. Let's not allow the promise of eternity to be so unreal and of so little worth to us that we're unwilling to suffer even the smallest bit of inconvenience for the sake of that promise. There is a promise of food that endures to eternal life. Let's work toward that food by being generous with what we have today.

The reason we give is that it properly responds to God and brings us closer to him. It allows us to become more like him. The promise we receive when we give is to know him more. The result when we give is that more people see God's character and are drawn to him. Giving both draws me and others to God. These things are full of grace and eternity.

Misunderstanding God's Response to Giving

One of the great hindrances to giving sacrificially is that our motivation doesn't flow from a proper understanding of grace or eternity. We're instead motivated by earthly desires, by a yearning to get our rewards now in earthly rather than eternal things. Simply put, we give to get more things now. But what if God had something better for us when we give sacrificially than a promise of more stuff? What if God is trying to rid us of all this earthly baggage so he can cultivate a genuine faith and trust in him? What if he wants to give us more of himself? What if he wants to bring us to a place where we are free to follow him?

Let me tell you how I've often confused my understanding of God's response to our sacrificial generosity. Each year around Christmas my parents give each of my children some money to give away. The only requirement is that the child must write a letter to their grandparents telling them what they did with the money. One year, my oldest son decided that he would give his money to help a friend of ours build a water well in East Africa. He was so excited about this project that he added some of his money to the gift. Seeing this heart in him and wanting to encourage his generosity, my wife and I told him we'd contribute to the well in an equal amount to whatever he gave. This is when it got interesting.

After I told my son our plan, he looked at me and said, "How much more do they need to complete the well?" I told him the amount, which was significantly more than he had considered giving away, and he asked me, "How much do I have in savings?" As I told him, I watched his mind churn. Suddenly, he looked up and said, "You said you would match whatever I gave, right?" "Yes," I now nervously replied. Then he said something that floored me, "If I give all of my money (including his savings) and you match it, we can complete the well. Right?"

He was right.

Keep in mind this was a fourteen-year-old kid giving away his life savings—which he was saving to buy a car in two years—to build a well in Africa.

After my son made this gift, I prayed God would use this gift to grow my son's faith; that God would make this gift a beacon of my son's faith for the rest of his life. What I meant was—grow his faith by providing him a car. Miraculously. That way he could correlate the thing he gave up with the thing he got back.

A few months after my son made this gift, the Holy Spirit transformed him. The kind of change that had no explanation. He became a different child. He was consumed with God's Word; he began desiring to honor his parents; he became a peacemaker with his siblings; he began sharing the gospel every chance he had. It was remarkable. One morning after this transformation while I was still praying God would use the gift to increase his faith—you know, get him a car—God stopped me and said, "I've already answered your prayer." I broke down.

I wept. Of course, he had. He answered it beyond my wildest dreams. He claimed the heart of my child. He gave my son more of himself. What more could I want? Why would I want God to "bless" him with something ephemeral (a car that would be trash in less than a decade) when the blessing he received is eternal.

When we grasp what God offers, when we follow him by giving sacrificially, we both forge and display a proper understanding of grace and eternity. And we give meaning to our diligent work and more simple lifestyle. We give passion to our pursuit of the things of Jesus and his path. All of it ends in deeper intimacy with Jesus.

WHAT IS SACRIFICIAL GIVING?

Before we conclude this chapter, you may wonder what I mean by sacrificial giving. I won't attempt to give hard and fast rules here either but I will say that for giving to be sacrificial (in our context) it'll almost certainly go beyond normal expectations. Sacrificial giving involves giving to things in such a way that our current or future plans are altered and changed.

It's easier to see than explain. In other words, you'll know it when you see it, and it isn't the same for everyone. The reason it's hard to identify sacrificial giving is most of our giving ministries focus on getting people to give out of their abundance. Rarely are people challenged to give up something they need (or think they need) for the sake of others. I'm all for helping people give more, but merely increasing the amount given doesn't make a gift sacrificial. We've defined generosity based on the amount given, instead of based on a heart of total surrender. As a result, we hardly know what it means to give sacrificially.

We all know about the widow who gives away her last mite (Mark 12:41–44; Luke 21:1–4). Jesus calls her generous. More so than all the others who give out of their abundance, she gives out of her poverty. Being sacrificial in our giving means considering the broader needs of the church and the vulnerable and how to testify to the worthiness of knowing God through our lives. Being sacrificial in our giving means we consider our lifestyle and determine where we can live more simply to increase our giving whenever God leads us. It means instead of asking how much we can afford to give, we're asking what's it going to take; we're asking how we might meet the needs that are present and known to us in whatever way possible. Even to our detriment.

I'm convinced the only reason we should play it safe with our resources is just in case God doesn't fulfill his promises. How's that for bad theology? Are you willing to stand before God and say the reason you didn't live more simply or give more sacrificially is that you wanted to make sure you had enough in case he quit providing? God never rebukes someone for relying on him too much. Trusting God too much isn't possible. This isn't reckless stupidity; it's using what God's given us for his glory and kingdom. It's refusing to view life through a temporary lens and choosing to put on a grace-filled, eternal one. It's freely following in the joyful way of Jesus.

SOMETHING NEEDS TO CHANGE

These three perspectives—working diligently, living simply, giving sacrificially—are inseparable. Each informs the others. When one gets out of whack, abuses and disillusionment occur. Living simply without giving sacrificially leads to hoarding. Giving sacrificially without working diligently or living simply leads to financial stress and irresponsibility. Working diligently without living simply or giving sacrificially leads to excess and greed. We need each perspective to help us follow Jesus.

I think we can all admit something needs to change in our lives. The question we have to wrestle with is, are we willing to work diligently, live simply, and give sacrificially for others? Are we willing to give up these otherwise good things to love our neighbors? The danger is that when we keep these things to the detriment of the people whom God commands us to care for, they become the testimony of our lives.

Let's close this chapter with a stunning example of these perspectives exemplified. C. T. Studd, George Müller, and Hudson Taylor are three well-known Christians who lived at the end of the nineteenth century. Each of these men made a determination to trust God by keeping nothing above their current needs and giving the rest away. They worked tirelessly for the sake of God's glory and lived as simply as possible. Any time extra money came into their hands they sought God's direction and got it moving for his purposes. Each man is remembered for his unusual trust in God and provision for others. What's so amazing about these three men is how God used each of them to meet the needs of the others in times of need. There is a circularity of provision that God orchestrated among them.

C. T. Studd gave away a good portion of his inheritance to George Müller. Müller was one of the biggest supporters of Hudson Taylor's missionary work in China. Taylor supported Studd as one of his missionaries in China. And the circle continued. Each man supported the others at different times and in different places. Resources were shared and needs were met when the needs were ripe. Instead of hoarding, each man trusted that God would provide in a time of need. And he did.

Our use of God's resources toward his ends is a natural part of the life of a follower of Jesus. In this flow, we see the goodness of life following God. We enter times of providing for our brothers and sisters only to be followed by times of receiving provision from them. Everyone contributes and receives. As a result, there ought to be no needy person among God's people. As Paul encourages the Corinthians, "your abundance at the present time should supply their need, so that their abundance may supply your need, that there may be fairness" (2 Cor. 8:14). This flow only happens when we step into the circle. When we give sacrificially and faithfully. Too many of us live so that we can always be the giver. Perhaps that's not the way God intended it. When we refuse to step into the circle, the flow stops, our money piles up and it rots in our hands. Those in need go without and those with abundance dry up spiritually. We're designed to live in community dependent on each other. Not one group dependent on another group, but each person dependent on each other.

This lifestyle of diligent work, simple living, and sacrificial generosity is the best we can live. It results in an intimacy with Jesus leading to unadulterated joy. Do you ever look at the lives of people trusting God completely and knowing him intimately, and feel sorry for them? They may go through challenging times, they may struggle with things, but we don't look at their lives and think, "I feel so sorry for them and their lives of trusting, knowing, and walking with God."

We'll never feel sorry for trusting God too much. This is an invitation to joy. Giving up certain lifestyle comforts or sacrificing for the sake of others may feel like death. And in many ways it is death, because you're dying to things you need to die to. But the end is life and joy.

There will never be a time when we're sorry for the things we lose to follow God. Look at all of the people we've considered—the disciples, Paul, the early church, the missionaries, the martyrs. They all had joy. They all had peace. They all lived lives we desire. They weren't special people, they were simply people who responded and said, "I'll take God at his word and live the life he has promised." This is the promise. This is what we're called into. This is the narrow path.

CHAPTER
TEN

FINDING OUR LIVES

WHEN JESUS TELLS us the high cost of following him, he includes an enticing promise with it.

Life.

The paradox is that the way to this life is through a death. We must take up our crosses, deny ourselves, and follow Jesus. This involves death to self—our pursuit of the world and any attempt to save ourselves. But, as we've seen, every death in God's order is followed by resurrection. While our old life dies, our new life begins. We die to live. This is the life I'm calling us to.

Paul willingly gave everything in this life for Christ. As he wrote to the Philippians, "I count everything as loss because of the surpassing worth of knowing Christ Jesus my Lord" (Phil. 3:8). Knowing Jesus was infinitely valuable to Paul, even when it entailed suffering for Jesus. We should all long for a holy desperation to know Jesus. Whatever the cost.

Knowing God is what we're promised when we follow Jesus. Whether through suffering, hardship, sacrifice or need, he promises to give us more of himself. Can we plead with God to take anything out of our lives that keeps us from knowing him more, including our comfortable lives? And to put anything into our lives that help us know him more, including suffering and hardship?

For some, this might sound admirable but impossible. Isn't this setting the bar too high? The reality is, when Jesus calls us to follow him it's because we're going the wrong way, carrying a load and baggage we aren't meant to carry. For many of us, instead of dropping our load and turning, we try to be a better version of ourselves, increasing our burden and baggage. After a while of bearing this burden, we become frustrated and discouraged. But I have good news—this isn't the call. The call is to stop, put down our burden, turn around, and start following Jesus. Instead of trying to be a better version of ourselves, we're called to reflect Jesus. To live as he lived and walk as he walked.

We can't do this alone. We must be yoked to Jesus by faith. We must walk with him in such a way that we're driven by love and the desire to know him more. It begins with turning and following him. The most essential condition for following Jesus is being with him. We can't know someone if we aren't with them. We may know about them, but we won't know them. This means that to follow Jesus, we must be with Jesus.

This is the only way to know him more, which leads to treasuring him more and putting him first in our lives. Once we do this, we begin to see with eternal

lenses. The way we view people and possessions radically transforms. From here we can finally love the way
Jesus loved and care the way Jesus cared, pursuing the
things Jesus loves. This isn't an increased burden to
bear, it's a work of Christ we're drawn to. It's the most
natural thing in the world, but we must get on the path.
We must rid ourselves of the world's baggage. We must
begin our eternal walk with Jesus here and now.

This is a call to be with Jesus—a call to come close
to him, experience him, and know him. This book is
intended to awaken us and see all the places where we
pursue things other than God. Don't be content any
longer to sip on the poison of this world. It leads to death
every time. God made this world good, but the only way
we can rightly enjoy it is when we're following Jesus.

HUNGERING FOR GOD

There seems to be a general angst among Christians
concerning the state of Christianity in the United
States. Oddly, this discontent hasn't seemed to awaken
an individual discontent in our spiritual walks. We
seem all too willing to complain about problems with
the church, but quite unwilling to fight for depth in
our spiritual lives. Could it be that the problems in the
church are deeply rooted in our lack of hunger for God?

Are you hungry to know Jesus? Are you willing
to strive to know him more? If you aren't longing for
more of Jesus, then something's not right. Get on your
knees and plead with God to change this. Keep coming
back to him no matter how long it takes. A. W. Tozer
beautifully frames this when he writes,

We have been snared in the coils of a spurious logic which insists that if we have found Him we need no more seek Him.... Come near to the holy men and women of the past and you will soon feel the heat of their desire after God. They mourned for Him, they prayed and wrestled and sought for Him day and night, in season and out, and when they had found Him the finding was all the sweeter for the long seeking.[1]

We can't truly seek God without pursuing hard after him. To think we can, is to make God into a trinket or bauble which we snag to adorn our lives at our whim and fancy. Jesus tells us his path is hard. It takes work.

Enter by the narrow gate. For the gate is wide and the way is easy that leads to destruction, and those who enter by it are many. For the gate is narrow and the way is hard that leads to life, and those who find it are few. (Matt. 7:13–14)

The path Jesus invites us to is narrow and hard. This is consistent with everything we have seen in the call of Jesus. This is what the rich young man felt. The world tells us that the path is easy and wide and we shouldn't have to work to follow Jesus. This is a horrendous lie. Following Jesus requires us to strive hard and pursue knowing him, whatever the cost. And there is a cost. The path is better—true. The burden is lighter—without a doubt. The end is life—hallelujah.

---

1. A. W. Tozer, *The Pursuit of God* (Harrisburg, PA: Christian Publications, 1948), chap. 1, Kindle.

But that doesn't mean the way is easy. Jesus tells us the way is narrow and hard, so much so that few find it. This should make us pause and consider whether we're on the narrow path. Or better yet, whether we're willing to pay the price to follow Jesus on this narrow path.

Are you willing to walk the hard path? How much do you want to know Jesus? If you don't want to know him more, then you might consider whether you know him at all. This following and longing after God isn't an optional add-on for super Christians, it's the central marker of a follower of Jesus. It's the watermark of faith.

Quit sitting around thinking this is going to magically happen to you one day. It won't. Jesus tells us that we have to pick up our crosses in this walk, that we have to choose the hard, narrow way. We must turn from the easy way—from a love of the world—and get to work striving toward Jesus. We need a holy discontent with our spiritual lives and with being satisfied with anything other than more of Jesus. We need to fight with every ounce of our souls to be near Jesus. To follow and know him.

There is only one way this happens—intentional pursuit.

Let's finish our journey by examining the central practices for pursuing Jesus on his narrow path.

PURSUING GOD

In Romans, Paul says, "Do not be conformed to this world, but be transformed by the renewal of your mind, that by testing you may discern what is the will of God, what is good and acceptable and perfect" (Rom. 12:1–2). We must oppose the incessant pull of the world that tries to make us look like it. Instead, we must actively renew our minds in concert with the Holy Spirit. When we do this, instead of being conformed to the world, we're transformed into people who can discern God's will.

Renewal and transformation come through the intentionality with which we order our days. Are we intentionally feeding ourselves with spiritual food or passively consuming earthly food?

If we're to walk with Jesus, that necessarily means we'll spend time with him. Do you spend purposeful, regular, and worshipful time with God in a meaningful way? What would your spiritual life look like if you gave it the attention you give to television, social media, fantasy sports, gaming, friends, shopping, or family? Are you regularly getting alone with God? If you aren't, I beg you to start. Get a Bible, journal, and pen. Get on your knees and start getting to know him.

William Paulsell expresses the intentionality we need in following God well:

> It is unlikely that we will deepen our relationship with God in a casual or haphazard manner. There will be a need for some intentional commitment and some reorganization in our own lives. But there is nothing that will enrich our lives more than a deeper and clearer perception of God's presence in the routine of daily living.[2]

---

2. William Paulsell, "Ways of Prayer: Designing a Personal Rule," *Weavings* 2, no. 5 (November–December 1987): 40.

The only way we'll get to know God is by making time with him the most important thing we do every day, ruthlessly eliminating distractions that prevent us from doing so. This won't happen by accident. We must make it a priority. If we want to follow Jesus, we must make it a priority to walk with him.

When we do this, the most remarkable thing happens—our love for God grows. Isaiah 44:3 says, "For I will pour water on the thirsty land, and streams on the dry ground; I will pour my Spirit upon your offspring, and my blessing on your descendants." God pours himself on us when we're thirsty for him. Will you drink deeply from the infinite well that is our God? When we do, our dry ground becomes a rushing river that springs life.

Are you willing to plead to increase this hunger and thirst? Will you get in your prayer closet and beg God to make you hungry and thirsty for him? Hunger is a gracious gift God gives those who seek him and seek him earnestly. This isn't a one-time off-handed prayer. This is a willingness to repeatedly come to God's throne, pleading for him to make himself known to us in such a way that all our longings and all our desires are transformed completely. He may not give us this immediately. He may refine us in our coming and wean us of our misplaced belief in our power to make ourselves hungry and thirsty. But if we persist in our coming, we won't be denied.

I'm reminded of a brilliant scene from the book *The Pilgrim's Progress* where Hopeful is recounting to Christian how he came to know God. He tells of coming to believe that he was a sinner in desperate need of the righteousness of Jesus and how he came to the throne of God in repentance and seeking:

> CHRISTIAN. *And did you [come to the throne in prayer] as you were bidden?*
>
> HOPEFUL. *Yes; over, and over, and over.*
>
> CHRISTIAN. *And did the Father reveal his Son to you?*
>
> HOPEFUL. *No, not at first, nor second, nor third, nor fourth, nor fifth; no, nor at the sixth time neither.*
>
> CHRISTIAN. *What did you do then?*
>
> HOPEFUL. *What! why I could not tell what to do.*
>
> CHRISTIAN. *Had you no thoughts of leaving off praying?*
>
> HOPEFUL. *Yes; and a hundred times twice told.*
>
> CHRISTIAN. *And what was the reason you did not?*
>
> HOPEFUL. *I believed that it was true which hath been told me, to wit, that without the righteousness of this Christ, all the world could not save me; and therefore, thought I with myself, if I leave off, I die, and I can but die at the throne of grace. And withal, this came into my mind, "If it tarry, wait for it; because it will surely come, and will not tarry."*

[Habakkuk 2:3] So I continued praying until the Father showed me his Son.[3]

What inspiring steadfastness and resolve. What beautiful understanding of the goodness of striving after God. Are you convinced that a life following Jesus is worth the toil? Will you come to the throne of grace *until* God shows you himself in all his glory? Until you hunger and thirst for nothing else besides him? Will you devote as much time as needed to make this a reality in your life? Neither seeking nor following Jesus is a passive endeavor. If we want more of Jesus, we must be with Jesus. This might not come naturally at first. Fight for it. Certainly, if he is worth knowing, he is worth pursuing to know.

There are many spiritual disciplines we can pursue which will help us know Jesus more and walk in his way. We discover these by both reading what Jesus tells us to do and examining what Jesus did. Thus, we establish an order of life through the study of Jesus's words and the observance of his practices. One thing abundantly clear in a study like this is Jesus didn't pursue these practices haphazardly or casually. He tackled them with fervor and consistency. They established the cadence of his life. From withdrawing regularly for solitude and prayer, to attending the synagogue and studying the Torah, to caring for the outcasts of society, Jesus's life and words were marked with consistent practices designed to cultivate a nearness to his Father.

---

3. John Bunyan, *The Pilgrim's Progress*, ed. Rosalie De Rosset (1678; repr., Chicago: Moody, 2007), 189–90.

If we're to pursue these practices, we must recognize that any attempt to add them to life as usual will end in frustration and failure. Therefore, we must be willing to reorder our lives to allow these practices to create its central cadence. Only then do we add the rest of life back in. Until we reorder our lives this way—until we hunger after God and in that hungering come to know him—the call to follow Jesus will produce sorrow and despair. We might obey, but it'll feel hard. However, through pursuing, obeying, and knowing God, God will do the impossible. He'll move us from sorrow to joy in our pursuit. He'll move us into a life that is free to follow him. As we come to him earnestly and persistently, he'll do his work in us.

Even though God is the one who ultimately moves us from sorrow to joy, we're still called to walk as Jesus walk. To commit the necessary intensity, focus, and prioritization of his practices. Only then will they take root and have their intended effects. Dallas Willard, in writing about first coming to this realization about spiritual practices, wrote this,

> I did not understand the intensity with which [spiritual disciplines] must be done, nor that the appropriate intensity required that they be engaged in for lengthy periods of undistracted time on a single occasion. Moreover, one's life as a whole had to be arranged in such a way that this would be possible. … [O]ne cannot tack an effective, life-transforming practice of prayer and study onto "life as

usual." Life as usual must go. It will be replaced by something far better.[4]

With these things in mind, let's explore three of the most central spiritual practices for forming our lives as Christ's followers: meditation, prayer, and obedience.[5]

MEDITATION

Don't freak out with the word "meditation." I'm not talking about sitting cross-legged and humming. What I mean by meditation is intentionally and intently focusing on God and who he is. As Dallas Willard explains,

> *If anyone is to love God and have his or her life filled with that love, God in his glorious reality must be brought before the mind and kept there in such a way that the mind takes root and stays fixed there.*[6]

There are a few ways to do this, but the most common are reading the Bible and withdrawing in silence and solitude. I'm cheating a little here by using the word "meditation" to refer to three different but related spiritual practices. But each of these practices helps us fix

---

4. Dallas Willard, *The Divine Conspiracy: Rediscovering Our Hidden Life in God* (New York: HarperCollins, 1997), 356.

5. There are many other practices that are important as well, but we don't have space to dive deeply. For a deeper look at these and other spiritual disciplines, see Richard J. Foster, *Celebration of Discipline: The Path to Spiritual Growth*, special anniversary ed. (San Francisco: HarperOne, 2018) and Donald S. Whitney, *Spiritual Disciplines for the Christian Life*, rev. and updated ed. (Colorado Springs, CO: NavPress, 2014).

6. Willard, *The Divine Conspiracy*, 324.

our attention on God. They allow us to do what Paul exhorts us to do in his letter to the Philippians,

> *Finally, brothers, whatever is true, whatever is honorable, whatever is just, whatever is pure, whatever is lovely, whatever is commendable, if there is any excellence, if there is anything worthy of praise, think about these things.* (Phil. 4:8)

Paul tells us to fix our minds on God and meditate on the things true of him. Who else fits each of these descriptors perfectly? God is perfectly true, honorable, just, pure, lovely, commendable, and worthy of praise, and we see these truths throughout Scripture. As a result, the first place we go to focus our minds on God is the Bible. It is, after all, God's revelation to us and the source from which we test everything else. We can be certain when we meditate on the Bible that we're meditating on who God has revealed himself to be.

The best practice for meditating on God's Word is withdrawing in silence and solitude. Jesus did this regularly during his earthly ministry. Silence and solitude allow us to clear our minds and sit and savor the person of Jesus Christ. Without this practice, we won't fully fix our attention and awareness on the person of God.

The ways we implement this practice will vary throughout our days, weeks, months, and years, but it should begin with a daily practice of time alone with God. Find a secluded quiet place, inside your home or elsewhere, and get alone with God. From there we grow to periodically spending entire days alone with God, eventually striving for multiple consecutive days alone with God in silence and solitude. If Jesus needed forty days of silence and solitude to prepare for ministry, then surely we could use a few days from time to time.

Meditating on God and his Word will guide us to a deeper knowledge of God and enlarge our view of him and his goodness. As Thomas Aquinas said, "Love … is born of an earnest consideration of the object loved."[7] I can't overstate the importance of meditation for our maturity in following Jesus. Simply put, if we want to follow Jesus, we must fix our attention on him, and meditation is the pathway to that end. Get alone and get with God.

PRAYER

Prayer is another central practice in the lives of followers of Jesus. Our hearts naturally turn to prayer and praise, as we meditate on God and his Word. It bubbles up and out of our hearts. If you study church history, you'll find the people who look the most like Christ are people of prayer, people with calloused knees and burdened hearts. Prayer cultivates humility and trust unlike anything else we do.

When we appeal to God in prayer, we're declaring we can't do it on our own and need his help. When we don't appeal to God in prayer, we're declaring we don't need him. As Andrew Murray says, "we are far more occupied with our work than we are with prayer. We believe more in speaking to men than we believe in

---

7. Saint Thomas Aquinas, *Summa Theologica*, vol. III–part II, second section (New York: Cosimo, 1912), 1300.

speaking to God."[8] Is our work of such a nature that we don't need God's help? Are we not seeking the salvation of souls and the healing of hearts? Without prayer, we're powerless to take part in this kind of eternal work.

Prayer is the most powerful ministry we have. Do you know what the only thing Jesus's disciples asked him to teach them to do was? Pray. They didn't ask him to teach them to heal, cast out demons, feed thousands with a few loaves and fish, walk on water, raise people from the dead, preach, or anything else. They asked him to teach them how to pray. Isn't that remarkable? Why was this the thing they wanted to learn most? It's because prayer was the single most powerful thing they saw him do. They couldn't fathom having access directly to the Father. They knew this access changed everything. And they wanted it.

Do you see prayer this way? Do you know that prayer involves the working of the Father, Son, and Holy Spirit? Every person of the godhead works in prayer, and we're invited into God's throne room to participate in this. When we enter this reality, it changes us. We come face to face with a real God who hears and reacts to our pleadings. Prayer isn't some polite memorized recitation—though this can be a fruitful practice. It's a raw outpouring of emotions and groanings, pleading with God to do the things he has promised to do. Praying isn't pretty. It's bold and unashamed while being reverent and submissive. This boldness with God teaches us to be bold with men—to be bold in following

8. Murray, *Absolute Surrender*, 42.

Jesus. Jesus came boldly before God's throne because he knew God. We too can come boldly before God's throne when we know him. This is where meditation and prayer overlap, and why they often go together in our lives.

Prayer changes us. But it must be real. It must be raw. And its power must be believed.

I encourage you to set some bold intentions in your daily practices of meditation and prayer. If you aren't doing these regularly, I want you to begin now. Set aside meaningful time each day for them. If you start with just a few minutes and something goes wrong, you entirely lose that time. Don't say to God, "I'll start by giving you scraps and hope to grow into a full meal." Start with a full meal. Reorder your life to make this *the* top priority of each day. The thing you won't miss. I know this advice goes against most spiritual self-help books, but if knowing God is important to you then that pursuit should be reflected on your calendar. You wouldn't offer your spouse a few minutes a day and think they'd be okay with that. Why would you offer God the same thing and think he's pleased? Give him your best. Every day.

If you don't think you have this much time to devote to knowing God, look at how you spend your time. My guess is you spend meaningful time each day doing something on your phone or television that is pure diversion. If you think you need this time to unwind instead of feasting on God, don't you think time in God's presence will do infinitely more good to calm your soul than a television show or social media feed? Meditation and prayer are the food that will feed your soul through the rest of your life. Commit to these practices daily and watch how God grows you as his apprentice in every area of your life. Watch as you begin to look more and more like Jesus.

OBEDIENCE

This last practice that we'll look at is less of a practice and more of a natural progression in the order of our lives. After Paul tells the Philippians to train their minds on things that are true, honorable, just, pure, lovely, commendable, and worthy of praise, he says, "What you have learned and received and heard and seen in me—practice these things, and the God of peace will be with you" (Phil. 4:9). The progression for Paul is to train our attention on the things of God and then do the things we saw him do. Not surprisingly, the things Paul did are the same things Jesus did. So, this last practice focuses on doing the things we've been told to do and saw Jesus and the apostles do. It's about adopting the lifestyle Jesus taught about and modeled.

I love this quote I heard in a sermon from Charlie Dates, "You cannot claim that you know God when you don't keep his commands and you cannot claim to keep his commands when you don't even know what his commands are."[9] Dates perfectly summarizes the intersection of what we've been discussing in this chapter. We must know what we're told to do if we're to do

---

9. Charlie Dates, "A Hard Word for a Soft Church," November 7, 2019, Chicago, Progressive Baptist Church, YouTube, 44:50, https://www.youtube.com/watch?v = n5TvO1y1zgc.

it, and we must do what we're told to do if we want
to call ourselves followers of Jesus. The way we know
what we're to do comes through meditation and prayer,
and the natural outflow of those practices is obedience.
The simple truth is that we won't fully understand the
truths in this book—about the joys found in a life of
walking with God—until we start obeying them. As
Gary Hoag says, "You don't figure it out until you live it
out that his commands on money are not crazy but are
for our good and his glory."

Whenever people start talking about things Christians *should* do, there seems to follow a crescendo of
accusation around legalism. I don't dismiss the danger
that exists for us to drift into legalism when pursuing
a life of obedience to God's commands. The commands
can quickly become our safety valve. This isn't the
point I'm trying to make. I'm not looking to create rules
you need to follow. What I want to highlight is the
unavoidable conclusion that our lack of obedience is
rooted in our lack of hunger for God. Our lack of desire
to be near God. Desire and obedience can look different
for people, but what it can't look like is apathy. There
needs to be passion, love, and desire to follow Jesus. A
hunger to know *and* obey. So, obedience isn't about a
new list of rules, it's about encountering and loving a
person—and then acting accordingly.

Besides, following Jesus is the best thing we can do,
not because of what we get out of it, but because it brings
God glory. My obedience stems from who he is, not what
I expect to get from it. This type of obedience can only
follow once we've trained our attention on him and have

come to know him through silence, solitude, and prayer. Only after this do we begin to glimpse his infinite worth. And his infinite worth drives us to obedience regardless of what happens to us. We walk as he walked and do what he did, because it displays and declares his glory.

This is why obedience isn't legalism. It's also how we remember that obedience won't save us. All of this points back to God and his glory. When we begin to walk in this way, our loves and lives are transformed. This is where we see "that new man, the new creature, that divine nature, that spirit which is born of the Spirit, that transformation into the image of Christ, that putting on of Christ, that workmanship created in us by God for good work, that Scripture describes."[10] This is where we see the effects of following Jesus. We become more like him with every step. We move toward holiness and righteousness. Our lives are consumed with knowing Jesus and making him known. This is the life of an apprentice. A life lived following Jesus.

And so we practice obedience. We become doers of the word, not merely hearers.

THAT I MIGHT NOT LOITER ON MY WAY TO HEAVEN

Returning to Philippians, Paul tells us that when we train our eyes on God and practice the things we see and now know, "the God of peace will be with [us]" (Phil. 4:9). The end is more of God, which leads to both

---

10. John Owen, *The Glory of Christ*, abridged by R. J. K. Law (1684; repr., Carlisle, PA: The Banner of Truth Trust, 1994), 88. He cites John 3:6; Rom. 6:3–8; 2 Cor. 3:18; 5:17; Eph. 4:20–24; 2 Pet. 1:4.

joy and peace. This is the promise of John 15:7 and Psalm 37:4. When we abide in God and let his words abide in us and when we delight in simply being near God, our desire for more of God grows and he gives us more of himself.

David Brainerd, a missionary accustomed to hardship and difficulty, sums up this desire well:

When I really enjoy God, I feel my desires of him the more insatiable, and my thirsting after holiness the more unquenchable; ... Oh, for holiness! Oh, for more of God in my soul! Oh, this pleasing pain! It makes my soul press after God. ... Oh, that I might not loiter on my heavenly journey![11]

This is the call of this book: that we would become people who are discontent with loitering in following Jesus, willing to run long and hard after Jesus on the narrow path, and willing to lose our lives for the sake of Jesus. No matter the cost.

This burning in our soul will draw us deeper into the way of Jesus. It will lead us to love as he loved, walk as he walked, and live as he lived. Psalm 16:11 gives us the hoped-for promise: "You make known to me the path of life; in your presence there is fullness of joy; at your right hand are pleasures forevermore" (Ps. 16:11). On the narrow path, Jesus leads us to feasting and drinking on the abundance of his delights (Ps. 36:8).

---

11. Jonathan Edwards, ed. Norman Pettit, *The Life of David Brainerd* in *The Works of Jonathan Edwards*, vol. 7 (New Haven: Yale University Press, 1985), 186.

Will you lay down your love for the world and the yoke you're burdened with? Will you join me on this journey? It's a journey I've only begun walking in my life. I'm learning to follow and live as Jesus lived. But, as I've sought out the narrow path, the sorrow of Jesus's call has diminished and I've been overwhelmed with joy and peace from the Lord. I have a new desperation to be near him. And in this pursuit, he has given me more of himself. The more I get, the more I want. I desperately want this for you. I want you to see and savor Jesus. I want you to be free to follow!

God has promised a hundredfold return for his children. The only thing that can possibly pay a return like that is being in God's presence. He has promised himself to his children. Let's quit looking for the fulfillment of his promises in places that won't and can't satisfy. Let's start looking for it in the promise maker.

CONCLUSION

*"**WHY ARE YOU HOLDING** onto something for a future that is uncertain when the need before you is so certain?"*

This question that resonated with us so clearly during our trip to Africa, has radically disrupted our lives—in a good, challenging way. In reading this book, you may have wondered whether or not we did anything in response to this question. While I hesitate to tell this story because I don't want this to become about us, I think the rest of this story will encourage you. Not because we're doing it right—I can assure you we regularly fail—but because it shows God's tremendous grace. The point of this story is God allowing us and many of our friends to become participants in the story of redemption he's writing. The point of the story is God's glory alone.

After getting home from Africa, we spent a few months processing, praying, and seeking counsel. We determined to use our "barns" to help alleviate some of the spiritual and physical suffering we had seen. We called Crisis Aid (the organization who took us on our initial trip) and told them we wanted to help fund the purchase of a small compound in a small town in East Africa. This property consisted of eight to ten small rooms where mothers and children suffering from extreme malnutrition could go to recuperate after leaving the hospital. We were committed now. All that remained was acquiring the property, raising the rest of the funds, and rehabilitating the property.

This is when things got interesting.

Because of some red tape, we were unable to acquire the small compound. It seemed as if we'd have to start over. However, in God's providence, there was another piece of property in the same area that was a perfect site to build a rehabilitation center and clinic. The catch was it cost twice as much. That was money we didn't have and weren't sure we could raise. But we were in; we'd trust God to provide the funding because it was outside of our capacity. Within a few weeks, Crisis Aid received an unsolicited donation for half of the cost to build the clinic and rehabilitation center. That meant we just had to fund and raise funds for the other half. God had answered the prayer almost before we began praying it.

As we set out to raise funding for the other half of this clinic, the generosity of our family and friends overwhelmed us. In a relatively short amount of time, we had received the funds for the clinic. God was faithful even as we imperfectly trusted he would be.

As construction began and more people learned about the project, excitement grew. Before long, two different families had come alongside the project and given money to expand the clinic. What began as a one-story clinic and rehabilitation center, had now grown into a three-story, full-service hospital. It's now the largest hospital in the area. And it serves everyone who comes in—for free. It offers life-saving testing and treatment for people sick with all kinds of illnesses rarely seen (and mostly eradicated) in the United States. Most importantly, every soul who enters the doors hears the good news of the gospel.

What began as our tiny hope to build an eight- to ten-room rehabilitation center became a modern hospital. Our contribution didn't change, but God had bigger plans in mind. His contribution is never limited.

We learned an important lesson in giving. We can only give what we have, the rest is up to God to bless and multiply. Just like the boy who gives his meager lunch for Jesus to feed thousands, all we can give is what we have. The miracle happens when it gets out of our hands and into God's. As long as I'm clutching my resources, they can only be used for my purposes. When I release those resources into God's hand, only his power and authority can limit their use. In other words, their influence can be eternal and infinite. Is there any better use?

So that's the story of what transpired following our trip to Africa. The real truth is this—our story is still being written. We're still imperfect disciples and continually need to relearn the same lessons. We still feel the sorrow of the rich young man all too often. However, we know where our treasure is and we know what path will take us there. We've experienced an indescribable joy in obedience. I can't wait to see where this journey will lead for the remainder of our days on earth. More than that, I can't wait to see how this journey prepares and equips us to worship God in his glory for eternity. I'm certain that anything we "lose" on earth will seem like nothing more than a pile of rubbish when we see clearly for the first time. I want to live every moment of every day with that truth in mind. Don't you?

Will you join us as we begin this eternal walk?

DISCUSSION AND PRAYER GUIDE

CHAPTER 1:
ASHAMED OF THE GOSPEL

Discussion Questions

1. Have you ever felt ashamed of the gospel or the call of the gospel? How?

2. Whose response to the call to sell everything to gain eternity do you relate to most, the joyful man or the rich young man? In what way(s) do you relate?

3. Discuss Jesus's response to the rich young ruler walking away in Mark 10:15–30. How does this response encourage you to respond to Jesus's call to follow him more like the joyful man?

4. What would change in your life today if you took Jesus's invitation to lose your life and follow him more seriously?

Prayer

Father, I cannot unburden myself from the things of this world without you doing a work in my life. In my own ability, I will fail every time. Yet, I want to want to lay down my life and follow you with a willingness and readiness that has no borders. I want to leave behind whatever you want me to leave behind to follow you. Please do a work in my life that moves me to respond to your call to follow you like the joyful man. Do a work in my life in your power. Help me see eternity with your eyes. In Jesus's name, Amen.

CHAPTER 2:
CALL TO SURRENDER

Discussion Questions

1. What is different in your life because of the call of Jesus? Does this response correspond more closely to Jesus's first call or second call of Peter?

2. What change of perspective would you need to make to view Jesus's call to lose your life for what it really is—a call to save your soul and find your life? How would this change of perspective impact your daily life?

3. What things do you keep in your life that prevent you from loving Jesus and following him?

4. How can you move from focusing on what the call to lose your life costs you to focusing on what it saves you from and for?

Prayer

Father, too often I view your call of surrender as a call of sorrow instead of a call to joy. Forgive me for my narrow view of you and of eternity. Please help me to see the joy of becoming a new creation, the majesty of your grace, and your promise of saving my soul as the treasures of my life. Please help me to throw off anything that prevents me from loving you and following you. Thank you for your grace and forgiveness. Help me to understand what I have been saved from and to. I love you. In Jesus's name, Amen.

CHAPTER 3:
LIFE OF SURRENDER

Discussion Questions

1. Which of the attitudes of surrender do you find the easiest to practice in your life? Which do you find the hardest?

2. How do trust and dependence go together in your walk with God? Where have you exhibited trust and dependence on God most consistently? Where have you struggled to exhibit trust and dependence on God?

3. Do you find yourself emphasizing belief or obedience in your relationship with God? How can you better attach your belief and obedience together in your relationship with God?

4. What can you do this week to begin aligning your belief and obedience as you seek to follow Jesus?

Prayer

Father, I want to surrender my life to you and lay down everything that stands between me and you. Please help me to take the first and next steps of obeying you as I begin to step into a life of belief and faith. Help me to develop a trust and dependence on you that displays to all who see me a belief in your goodness and grace. I want to look more like Jesus every day and I want my life to consistently display the things I say I believe about you. Create in me a clean heart and mold me into the image of Jesus.

I am yours. One-hundred percent yours. Do with me as you wish. May glory come to your name in all things. In Jesus's name, Amen.

CHAPTER 4:
BIBLE'S WITNESS OF
FINANCIAL SURRENDER

Discussion Questions

1. How have you seen the Bible misused in teachings about money? How have you misused the Bible in understanding God's role for wealth and money in the lives of his followers?

2. Which of the overarching biblical themes on money did you find most surprising? How did it surprise you?

3. How do you balance the goodness of creation with all of the warnings around wealth and greed? How do you guard against extremes in your own life?

4. Did studying the Bible's witness of financial surrender change your view on how God wants you to view and handle your money? If so, how?

Prayer

Father, thank you for your creation. Thank you for the goodness of this world and the things in this world. Grant me the grace to be able to savor the beauty of your creation without ever putting it in your place. Help me to see the Creator whenever I am admiring the goodness of the creation. Please protect me from greed and covetousness and help me to identify and root out these sins wherever they lurk in my heart. Teach me to be content in any and every circumstance. Prepare my heart to hold my wealth loosely and use it for your glory in every decision I make. If my wealth keeps me from you in any way, take it. I want to put you first. Teach me to do just that. I need your grace to walk this path. Guide me. In Jesus's name, Amen.

CHAPTER 5:
LIFESTYLES OF JESUS AND
HIS EARLIEST FOLLOWERS

Discussion Questions

1. How do you think we should use the examples of the lives of Jesus, the disciples, and the earliest followers in shaping how we live today? Are they normative, aspirational, inspirational, or something else?

2. What conclusions can you draw (in addition to the ones I posed) from the lifestyles we examined? What specific changes do you want to make in your own life after examining these lives?

3. In light of these last two chapters, in what ways do you believe a follower of Jesus's lifestyle should look different than the world's?

4. Which of the misuses in teaching on money do you see most often? How can you work to avoid this kind of misuse in your own study of the Bible?

Prayer

Father, I desperately want to look like your Son in my life. I want to show the greatest love possible to my brothers and sisters in Christ and be willing to lay down my life for them. Show me every area of my life that does not look like your Son and give me the courage to set my yoke down and follow in the way of Jesus. I believe that a life following you is worth everything I have, including my life. Help me to live consistently with that belief. I want to want you more. Give me the strength to love you more each day. In Jesus's name, Amen.

CHAPTER 6: THE GREAT BARRIER

Discussion Questions

1. What are the ways you are prone to slide into a love for the world? How can you resist this tendency in your life?

2. How have you seen a love for the world make it harder for you to love God and obey him? How have you seen a love for the world move you toward enmity with God?

3. Which of the questions under the heading "How do I identify a love for the world?" hit closest to home? How can you move toward rooting out this love in your life?

Prayer

Father, I confess that a love for the world is a constant temptation for me which I fall prey to far too often. Help me to identify the places in my life where I exhibit a love for the world and give me your grace to root this love out of my heart. Replace this love of the world with a love of you and eternity. Give me eyes to see your creation for what it is—good and beautiful—but give me the grace to not put those good and beautiful things in the place where you alone belong. I want to love you more than the world and I ask for help in doing so. I need your help and I trust your promise to provide it. Be with me. Help me. In Jesus's name, Amen.

CHAPTER 7: CHRISTIANIZATION OF THE GREAT BARRIER

Discussion Questions

1. Should the church look like the world in its practices and pursuits? If not, why should it look different and how should it look different?

2. How have you seen an implied prosperity gospel appear in your church or in a majority of churches in the United States?

3. How can you define a "successful" church in a way that emphasizes the pursuit of God instead of the pursuit of the world? How can you help your church move toward these emphases?

4. Which of the noble-sounding justifications for loving the world have you seen most clearly in your own life? Do you agree with my assessment that these are (or can be) excuses we use to justify a life with more of the world where we don't have to trust God as much? Why or why not?

5. How do you intend to battle a love for the world in your life?

Prayer

Father, please help me to see all the places where I have inserted a love for the world in my life and the life of following you. Help me to identify where I am prone to make excuses to mask my love for the world because I am unwilling to trust you. I want to walk the narrow path and want to get rid of anything in my life that keeps me from that path. Please give me wisdom to discern between using the world for your glory and using the world for my own glory. I only want to bring glory to your name. In Jesus's name, Amen.

CHAPTER 8:
WITNESS OF OUR MONEY

Discussion Questions

1. How does an understanding of the spiritual and physical need in the world shape the way you view your money and resources? Did anything about the spiritual and physical needs of the world surprise you?

2. What does your usage of money say to the world about what you believe to be most important and urgent? If you don't like your answer to that question, how do you plan on changing your usage of money to better reflect what you believe to be most important and urgent?

3. Do you trust God as your provider? How do you demonstrate that trust in your life?

4. Would anyone look at the way you spend money and doubt you really believe there is an eternal reality awaiting us?

Prayer

Father, please forgive me for ignoring the spiritual and physical realities of the world. I long to use my money in a way that demonstrates that I trust you. In a way that demonstrates my belief in an eternal reality waiting for me. Give me your heart for the world and allow me to trust you in such a way that I can give freely to meet spiritual and physical needs in the world knowing that you will care for me. Help me to be less concerned for my

*wants and more concerned about the spiritual and phys-
ical needs in this world. Help me to use my money in a
way that points to you as the God who is trustworthy. In
Jesus's name, Amen.*

CHAPTER 9:
HOW THEN WILL WE LIVE?

Discussion Questions

1. Are you ready to put down your yoke and pick up
the yoke of Jesus? If so, commemorate that decision
with a tangible commitment personally or with a
group of people.

2. How do you live in the tension of working diligently
and the tendency of such work (in the United States)
to create an increase in income? What motivations
will you use for working diligently? What protections
will you put in place for dealing with an increase in
income?

3. What does it look like for you to live simply? What
are some simple steps you can take to enter into the
joy of a simple lifestyle?

4. How can you engage in sacrificial generosity in your
life? Why is sacrificial giving so important in the life
of a follower of Jesus?

5. What is going to change in your life so that you can
more fully follow Jesus?

Prayer

Father, I want my life to proclaim to others that you are trustworthy. I'm tired of carrying my own yoke and desire to carry yours. If there is any area of my life that does not honor you or bring you glory, I turn it over to you. Teach me to work diligently, live simply, and give sacrificially to your glory and not to my own. Let me not enter into these practices as a way to try to earn your approval or acceptance, but as a way to worship you and bring you glory. I admit that I'm a sinner who can't ever do enough to earn your grace and so any action I take in following you please receive as an act of worship and thanksgiving. I only want to honor you. Bring glory to your name through my life. In Jesus's name, Amen.

CHAPTER 10: FINDING OUR LIVES

Discussion Questions

1. How hard have you contended for a closer walk with Jesus in your life? Are you willing to hunger and thirst and strive to know Jesus more?

2. Which spiritual practices are a regular part of your life? Which ones do you want to make a more regular part of your life? How do you plan on doing this?

3. Spend time simply praying and crying out to God either alone or as a group.

4. What is one step of obedience you intend to take this next week in your journey of following Jesus?

Prayer

Father, I'm tired of loitering on my way to heaven. I'm tired of pursuing you with less than all of my heart, soul, mind, and strength. I want to give you my all, but something continues to hold me back. Whatever that thing is, I give it to you. Take it from me. I lay down my life at your feet. My life is yours, use me for whatever brings you glory. Help my hunger for you to grow with each new step I take. Give me the boldness and confidence to obey you in each new thing you put in my life. I want to be your apprentice and follow on the narrow path. I'm wholly yours. Take me. Use me. In Jesus's name, Amen.

NOTES

NOTES